Functional Thinking

Neal Ford

Beijing · Cambridge · Farnham · Köln · Sebastopol · Tokyo

Functional Thinking

by Neal Ford

Published by O'Reilly Media, Inc., 1005 Gravenstein Highway North, Sebastopol, CA 95472.

O'Reilly books may be purchased for educational, business, or sales promotional use. Online editions are also available for most titles (*http://my.safaribooksonline.com*). For more information, contact our corporate/institutional sales department: 800-998-9938 or *corporate@oreilly.com*.

Editors: Mike Loukides and Meghan Blanchette	**Indexer:** Judith McConville
Production Editor: Kristen Brown	**Cover Designer:** Karen Montgomery
Copyeditor: Eileen Cohen	**Interior Designer:** David Futato
Proofreader: Jasmine Kwityn	**Illustrator:** Rebecca Demarest

July 2014:   First Edition

Revision History for the First Edition:

2014-06-26:   First release

See *http://oreilly.com/catalog/errata.csp?isbn=9781449365516* for release details.

ISBN: 978-1-449-36551-6

[LSI]

Table of Contents

Preface

The first time I seriously looked at functional programming was in 2004. I became intrigued by alternative languages on the .NET platform, and started playing with Haskell and a few pre-F#, ML-based languages. In 2005, I did a conference talk named "Functional Languages and .NET" at a few venues, but the languages at the time were more proof-of-concept and toys than anything else. The possibilities of thinking within a new paradigm fascinated me, however, and changed the way I approached some problems in more familiar languages.

I revisited this topic in 2010 because I observed the rise of languages such as Clojure and Scala in the Java ecosystem and remembered the cool stuff from five years before. I started one afternoon on Wikipedia, following link after link, and was mesmerized by the end of the day. That started an exploration of numerous branches of thought in the functional programming world. That research culminated in the "Functional Thinking" talk, debuting in 2011 at the *33rd Degree Conference* (*http://33degree.org*) in Poland and the IBM developerWorks article series of the same name (*http://bit.ly/dev-works-ft-series*). Over the course of the next two years, I wrote an article each month on functional programming, which was a great way to establish and maintain a research and exploration plan. I continued delivering (and refining, based on feedback) the presentation until the present day.

This book is the culmination of all the ideas from the "Functional Thinking" talk and article series. I've found that the best way to hone material is to present it to audiences over and over, because I learn something new about the material every time I present or write about it. Some relationships and commonalities appear only after deep research and forced thought (deadlines are great focusers!).

My last book, *Presentation Patterns* (*http://presentationpatterns.com*), described the importance of visual metaphors in conference presentations. For *Functional Thinking*, I chose a blackboard and chalk theme (to invoke the mathematical connection to functional programming concepts). At the end of the presentation, as I talk about practical applications, I show a picture of a piece of chalk resting at the foot of a blackboard, metaphorically imploring viewers to pick it up and explore these ideas on their own.

My goal in the talk, the article series, and this book is to present the core ideas of functional programming in a way that is accessible to developers steeped in imperative, object-oriented languages. I hope you enjoy this distillation of ideas, and pick up the chalk and continue your own exploration.

—Neal Ford, Atlanta, June 2014

Chapter Overview

Each chapter in this book shows examples of functional thinking. Chapter 1, *Why*, provides a broad overview and shows some examples of the mental shift prevalent in the rest of the book. Chapter 2, *Shift*, describes the gradual process of shifting your perspective from that of an object-oriented, imperative programmer to that of a functional programmer. To illustrate the *shift* in thinking required, I solve a common problem in both imperative and functional styles. I then do an extensive case study, showing the way a functional perspective (and some helper syntax) can help *shift* you toward a functional mindset.

Chapter 3, *Cede*, shows examples of common chores you can now cede to your language or runtime. One of the "moving parts" described by Michael Feathers is *state*, which is typically managed explicitly in nonfunctional languages. Closures allow you to defer some state-handling to the runtime; I show examples of how that state handling mechanism works underneath. In this chapter, I show how functional thinking also allows you to cede details like accumulation to recursion, and impacts your granularity of code reuse.

Chapter 4, *Smarter, Not Harder*, focuses on two extended examples of *eliminating moving parts* by allowing the runtime to cache function results for you and implementing laziness. Many functional languages include *memoization* (either natively, via a library, or a trivial implementation), which handles a common performance optimization for you. I show an example, based on the *number classifier* example in Chapter 2, of several levels of optimization, both handwritten and via memoization. At the risk of giving away the ending, memoization wins. *Lazy* data structures, which defer calculation until necessary, allow you to think differently about data structures. I show how to implement lazy data structures (even in nonfunctional languages) and how to leverage laziness that already exists.

Chapter 5, *Evolve*, shows how languages are evolving to become more functional. I also talk about evolutionary language trends such as operator overloading and new dispatch options beyond just method calls, about bending your language toward your problem (not the other way around), and common functional data structures such as Option.

Chapter 6, *Advance*, shows examples of common approaches to problems. I show how design patterns change (or disappear) in the functional programming world. I also contrast code reuse via inheritance versus composition and discuss their explicit and implicit coupling points.

Chapter 7, *Practical Thinking*, shows specific long-anticipated functional features that recently appeared in the Java Developer Kit (JDK). I show how Java 8 fits in with the *functional thinking* from other languages, including the use of higher-order functions (i.e., lambda blocks). I also discuss some clever ways in which Java 8 maintains graceful backward compatibility, and I highlight the `Stream` API, which allows concise and descriptive workflows. And, finally, I show how Java 8 has added `Option` to eliminate potential `null` confusion. I also cover topics such as functional architecture and databases and how the functional perspective changes those designs.

Chapter 8, *Polyglot and Polyparadigm*, describes the impact of functional programming on the polyglot world we now live in; we increasingly encounter and incorporate numerous languages on projects. Many new languages are also *polyparadigm*, supporting several different programming models. For example, Scala supports object-oriented and functional programming. The last chapter discusses the pros and cons of living in a paradigmatically richer world.

Conventions Used in This Book

The following typographical conventions are used in this book:

Italic
> Indicates new terms, URLs, email addresses, filenames, and file extensions.

`Constant width`
> Used for program listings, as well as within paragraphs to refer to program elements such as variable or function names, databases, data types, environment variables, statements, and keywords.

`Constant width bold`
> Shows commands or other text that should be typed literally by the user.

`Constant width italic`
> Shows text that should be replaced with user-supplied values or by values determined by context.

 This icon signifies a tip, suggestion, or general note.

Using Code Examples

Supplemental material (code examples, exercises, etc.) is available for download at *https://github.com/oreillymedia/functional_thinking*.

This book is here to help you get your job done. In general, if example code is offered with this book, you may use it in your programs and documentation. You do not need to contact us for permission unless you're reproducing a significant portion of the code. For example, writing a program that uses several chunks of code from this book does not require permission. Selling or distributing a CD-ROM of examples from O'Reilly books does require permission. Answering a question by citing this book and quoting example code does not require permission. Incorporating a significant amount of example code from this book into your product's documentation does require permission.

We appreciate, but do not require, attribution. An attribution usually includes the title, author, publisher, and ISBN. For example: "*Functional Thinking* by Neal Ford (O'Reilly). Copyright 2014 Neal Ford, 978-1-449-36551-6."

If you feel your use of code examples falls outside fair use or the permission given above, feel free to contact us at *permissions@oreilly.com*.

Safari® Books Online

 *Safari Books Online* is an on-demand digital library that delivers expert content in both book and video form from the world's leading authors in technology and business.

Technology professionals, software developers, web designers, and business and creative professionals use Safari Books Online as their primary resource for research, problem solving, learning, and certification training.

Safari Books Online offers a range of product mixes and pricing programs for organizations, government agencies, and individuals. Subscribers have access to thousands of books, training videos, and prepublication manuscripts in one fully searchable database from publishers like O'Reilly Media, Prentice Hall Professional, Addison-Wesley Professional, Microsoft Press, Sams, Que, Peachpit Press, Focal Press, Cisco Press, John Wiley & Sons, Syngress, Morgan Kaufmann, IBM Redbooks, Packt, Adobe Press, FT Press, Apress, Manning, New Riders, McGraw-Hill, Jones & Bartlett, Course Technology, and dozens more. For more information about Safari Books Online, please visit us online.

How to Contact Us

Please address comments and questions concerning this book to the publisher:

O'Reilly Media, Inc.
1005 Gravenstein Highway North
Sebastopol, CA 95472
800-998-9938 (in the United States or Canada)
707-829-0515 (international or local)
707-829-0104 (fax)

We have a web page for this book, where we list errata, examples, and any additional information. You can access this page at *http://bit.ly/functional-thinking*.

To comment or ask technical questions about this book, send email to *bookques tions@oreilly.com*.

For more information about our books, courses, conferences, and news, see our website at *http://www.oreilly.com*.

Find us on Facebook: *http://facebook.com/oreilly*

Follow us on Twitter: *http://twitter.com/oreillymedia*

Watch us on YouTube: *http://www.youtube.com/oreillymedia*

Acknowledgments

Thanks to my family at ThoughtWorks, the best place of employment around, and to all my fellow speakers on the conference circuit, especially the No Fluff, Just Stuff speakers, against whom I've bounced many ideas. Thanks to all the people who have attended my "Functional Thinking" talks at conferences over the years—your feedback helped me hone this material. Special thanks to the technical reviewers on this book, who made outstanding substantive suggestions, especially the early readers who took the time to submit errata, many of which exposed subtle opportunities for clarification. Thanks to friends and family too numerous to mention who act as my incredible support network, especially John Drescher, who looks after the cats when we're away. And, of course, my long-suffering wife Candy, who long ago lost hope that I would ever stop doing this.

CHAPTER 1

Why

Let's say for a moment that you are a lumberjack. You have the best axe in the forest, which makes you the most productive lumberjack in the camp. Then one day someone shows up and extols the virtues of a new tree-cutting paradigm, the *chainsaw*. The sales guy is persuasive, so you buy a chainsaw, but you don't know how it works. Demonstrating your expertise with the previous tree-cutting paradigm, you swing it vigorously at a tree—without cranking it. You quickly conclude that this newfangled chainsaw is a fad, and you return to your axe. Then, someone appears and shows you how to *crank* the chainsaw.

The problem with a completely new programming paradigm isn't learning a new language. After all, everyone reading this has learned numerous computer languages—language syntax is merely details. The tricky part is learning to *think* in a different way.

This book explores the subject of functional programming but isn't really about functional programming languages. Make no mistake—I show lots of code, in numerous languages; this book is all about code. As I'll illustrate, writing code in a "functional" manner touches on design trade–offs, different reusable building blocks, and a host of other insights. Because I favor ideas over syntax, I start with Java, the most familiar baseline for the largest group of developers, and mix in both pre-Java 8 and Java 8 examples. As much as possible, I show functional programming concepts in Java (or close relatives) and move to other languages only to demonstrate unique capabilities.

Even if you don't care about Scala or Clojure, and are happy coding in your current language for the rest of your career, your language will change underneath you, looking more functional all the time. Now is the time to learn functional paradigms, so that you can leverage them when (not if) they appear in your everyday language. Let's take a look at the reasons why all languages are gradually becoming more functional.

Shifting Paradigms

Computer science often advances in fits and starts, with good ideas appearing decades before they suddenly become part of the mainstream. For example, Simula 67, created in 1967, is the first object-oriented language, yet object orientation didn't really become mainstream until after the popularization of C++, which first appeared in 1983. Often, good ideas await foundation technologies to catch up. In its early years, Java was regularly considered too slow and expansive in memory usage for high-performance applications, but shifts in the hardware market made it an attractive choice.

Functional programming follows the same conceptual trajectory as object orientation: developed in academia over the last few decades, it has slowly crept into all modern programming languages. Yet just adding new syntax to a language doesn't inform developers of the best way to leverage this new way of thinking.

I start with a contrast between the traditional programming style (imperative loops) and a more functional way of solving the same problem. For the problem to solve, I dip into a famous event in computer science history, a challenge issued from Jon Bentley, the writer of a regular column in *Communications of the ACM* called "Programming Pearls," to Donald Knuth, an early computer science pioneer. The challenge is common to anyone who has written text-manipulation code: *read a file of text, determine the most frequently used words, and print out a sorted list of those words along with their frequencies.* Just tackling the word-frequency portion, I write a solution in "traditional" Java, shown in Example 1-1.

Example 1-1. Word frequencies in Java

```java
public class Words {
    private Set<String> NON_WORDS = new HashSet<String>() {{
        add("the"); add("and"); add("of"); add("to"); add("a");
        add("i"); add("it"); add("in"); add("or"); add("is");
        add("d"); add("s"); add("as"); add("so"); add("but");
        add("be"); }};

    public Map wordFreq(String words) {
        TreeMap<String, Integer> wordMap = new TreeMap<String, Integer>();
        Matcher m = Pattern.compile("\\w+").matcher(words);
        while (m.find()) {
            String word = m.group().toLowerCase();
            if (! NON_WORDS.contains(word)) {
                if (wordMap.get(word) == null) {
                    wordMap.put(word, 1);
                }
                else {
                    wordMap.put(word, wordMap.get(word) + 1);
                }
            }
        }
        return wordMap;
```

```
        }
    }
```

In Example 1-1, I create a set of nonwords (articles and other "glue" words), then create the `wordFreq()` method. In it, I build a `Map` to hold the key/value pairs, then create a regular expression to allow me to determine words. The bulk of this listing iterates over the found words, ensuring that the actual word is either added the first time to the map or its occurrence is incremented. This style of coding is quite common in languages that encourage you to work through collections (such as regular expression matches) piecemeal.

Consider the updated version that takes advantage of the `Stream` API and the support for higher-order functions via lambda blocks in Java 8 (all discussed in more detail later), shown in Example 1-2.

Example 1-2. Word frequency in Java 8

```java
private List<String> regexToList(String words, String regex) {
    List wordList = new ArrayList<>();
    Matcher m = Pattern.compile(regex).matcher(words);
    while (m.find())
    wordList.add(m.group());
    return wordList;
}

public Map wordFreq(String words) {
    TreeMap<String, Integer> wordMap = new TreeMap<>();
    regexToList(words, "\\w+").stream()
            .map(w -> w.toLowerCase())
            .filter(w -> !NON_WORDS.contains(w))
            .forEach(w -> wordMap.put(w, wordMap.getOrDefault(w, 0) + 1));
    return wordMap;
}
```

In Example 1-2, I convert the results of the regular expression match to a stream, which allows me to perform discrete operations: make all the entries lowercase, filter out the nonwords, and count the frequencies of the remaining words. By converting the iterator returned via `find()` to a stream in the `regexToList()` method, I can perform the required operations one after the other, in the same way that I think about the problem. Although I could do that in the imperative version in Example 1-1 by looping over the collection three times (once to make each word lowercase, once to filter nonwords, and once to count occurrences), I know not to do that because it would be terribly inefficient. By performing all three operations within the iterator block in Example 1-1, I'm trading *clarity* for *performance*. Although this is a common trade-off, it's one I'd rather not make.

In his "Simple Made Easy" keynote (*http://www.infoq.com/presentations/Simple-Made-Easy*) at the Strange Loop conference, Rich Hickey, the creator of Clojure (*http://clojure.org*), reintroduced an arcane word, *complect*: to join by weaving or twining together; to interweave. Imperative programming often forces you to *complect* your tasks so that you can fit them all within a single loop, for efficiency. Functional programming via higher-order functions such as `map()` and `filter()` allows you to elevate your level of abstraction, seeing problems with better clarity. I show many examples of functional thinking as a powerful antidote to incidental complecting.

Aligning with Language Trends

If you look at the changes coming to all major languages, they all add functional extensions. Groovy has been adding functional capabilities for a while, including advanced features such as memoization (the ability for the runtime to cache function return values automatically). Even Java itself will finally grow more functional extensions, as lambda blocks (i.e., higher-order functions) finally appear in Java 8, and arguably the most widely used language, JavaScript, has numerous functional features. Even the venerable C++ added lambda blocks in the language's 2011 standard, and has generally shown more functional programming interest, including intriguing libraries such as the Boost.Phoenix library (*http://bit.ly/phoenix-library*).

Learning these paradigms now allows you to utilize the features as soon as they appear, either in your use of a new language such as Clojure or in the language you use every day. In Chapter 2, I cover how to *shift* your thinking to take advantage of these advanced facilities.

Ceding Control to the Language/Runtime

During the short history of computer science, the mainstream of technology sometimes spawns branches, either practical or academic. For example, in the 1990s, the move to personal computers saw an explosion in popularity of fourth-generation languages (4GL) such as dBASE, Clipper, FoxPro, Paradox, and a host of others. One of the selling points of these languages was a higher-level abstraction than a 3GL like C or Pascal. In other words, you could issue a single command in a 4GL that would take many commands in a 3GL because the 4GL already had more "prebaked" context. These languages were already equipped to read popular database formats from disk rather than force customized implementations.

Functional programming is a similar offshoot from academia, where computer scientists wanted to find ways of expressing new ideas and paradigms. Every so often, a branch will rejoin the mainstream, which is what is happening to functional programming now. Functional languages are sprouting not just on the Java Virtual Machine (JVM), where the two most interesting new languages are Scala and Clojure, but on the .NET platform as well, which includes F# as a first-class citizen. Why this embrace of functional programming by all the platforms?

Back in the early 1980s, when I was in university, we used a development environment called Pecan Pascal, whose unique feature was the ability to run the same Pascal code on either the Apple][or IBM PC. The Pecan engineers achieved this feat by using something mysterious called "bytecode." When the developer compiled his code, he compiled it to this "bytecode," which ran on a "virtual machine," written natively for each of the two platforms. And it was a hideous experience. The resulting code was achingly slow even for simple class assignments. The hardware at the time just wasn't up to the challenge.

Of course, we all recognize this architecture. A decade after Pecan Pascal, Sun released Java using the same techniques, straining but succeeding in mid-1990s hardware environments. It also added other developer-friendly features, such as automatic garbage collection. I never want to code in a non-garbage-collected language again. Been there, done that, got the T-shirt, and don't want to go back, because I'd rather spend my time at a higher level of abstraction, thinking about ways to solve complex business scenarios, not complicated plumbing problems. I rejoice in the fact that Java reduces the pain of explicit memory management, and I try to find that same level of convenience in other places.

 Life's too short for `malloc`.

Over time, developers cede more control over tedious tasks to our languages and runtimes. I don't lament the lack of direct memory control for the types of applications I write, and ignoring that allows me to focus on more important problems. Java eased our interaction with memory management; functional programming languages allow us to replace other core building blocks with higher-order abstractions.

Examples of replacing detailed implementations with simpler ones relying on the runtime to handle mundane details abound in this book.

Concision

Michael Feathers, author of *Working with Legacy Code*, captured a key difference between functional and object-oriented abstractions in 140 lowly characters on Twitter (*https://twitter.com/mfeathers/status/29581296216*):

> OO makes code understandable by encapsulating moving parts. FP makes code understandable by minimizing moving parts.
>
> — Michael Feathers

Think about the things you know about object-oriented programming (OOP) constructs: encapsulation, scoping, visibility, and other mechanisms exist to exert fine-grained control over who can see and change state. More complications pile up when you deal with state plus threading. These mechanisms are what Feathers referred to as "moving parts." Rather than build mechanisms to *control* mutable state, most functional languages try to *remove* mutable state, a "moving part." The theory follows that if the language exposes fewer potentially error-prone features, it is less likely for developers to make errors. I will show numerous examples throughout of functional programming eliminating variables, abstractions, and other moving parts.

In object-oriented imperative programming languages, the units of reuse are classes and the messages they communicate with, captured in a class diagram. The seminal work in that space, *Design Patterns: Elements of Reusable Object-Oriented Software* (by Erich Gamma, Richard Helm, Ralph Johnson, and John Vlissides), includes at least one class diagram with each pattern. In the OOP world, developers are encouraged to create unique data structures, with specific operations attached in the form of methods. Functional programming languages don't try to achieve reuse in quite the same way. In functional programming languages, the preference is for a few key data structures (such as `list`, `set`, and `map`) with highly optimized operations on those data structures. To utilize this machinery, developers pass data structures plus higher-order functions to plug into the machinery, customizing it for a particular use.

Consider a simplified portion of the code from Example 1-2:

```
regexToList(words, "\\b\\w+\\b").stream()
            .filter(w -> !NON_WORDS.contains(w))
```

To retrieve a subset of a list, call the `filter()` method, passing the list as a stream of values and a higher-order function specifying the filter criteria (in this case, the syntactically sugared `(w → !NON_WORDS.contains(w))`). The machinery applies the filter criteria in an efficient way, returning the filtered list.

Encapsulation at the function level allows reuse at a more granular, fundamental level than building new class structures for every problem. Dozens of XML libraries exist in the Java world, each with its own internal data structures. One advantage of leveraging higher-level abstractions is already appearing in the Clojure space. Recent clever innovations in Clojure's libraries have managed to rewrite the `map` function to be automatically parallelizable, meaning that all map operations get a performance boost without developer intervention.

Functional programmers prefer a few core data structures, building optimized machinery to understand them. Object-oriented programmers tend to create new data structures and attendant operations constantly—building new classes and messages between them is the predominant object oriented paradigm. Encapsulating all data structures within classes discourages reuse at the method level, preferring larger framework-style reuse. Functional programming constructs make it easier to reuse code at a more atomic level.

Consider the indexOfAny() method, from the popular Java framework Apache Commons (*http://commons.apache.org/proper/commons-lang*), which provides a slew of helpers for Java, in Example 1-3.

Example 1-3. indexOfAny() from Apache Commons StringUtils

```
// From Apache Commons Lang, http://commons.apache.org/lang/
public static int indexOfAny(String str, char[] searchChars) {
    if (isEmpty(str) || ArrayUtils.isEmpty(searchChars)) { ❶
        return INDEX_NOT_FOUND;
    }
    int csLen = str.length();                               ❷
    int csLast = csLen - 1;
    int searchLen = searchChars.length;
    int searchLast = searchLen - 1;
    for (int i = 0; i < csLen; i++) {                       ❸
        char ch = str.charAt(i);
        for (int j = 0; j < searchLen; j++) {       ❹
            if (searchChars[j] == ch) {             ❺
                if (i < csLast && j < searchLast && CharUtils.isHighSurrogate(ch)) {
                    if (searchChars[j + 1] == str.charAt(i + 1)) {
                        return i;
                    }
                } else {
                    return i;
                }
            }
        }
    }
    return INDEX_NOT_FOUND;
}
```

❶ Safety checks

❷ Initialization

❸ Outer iteration

❹ Inner iteration

❺ Decisions, decisions, decisions

The IndexofAny() method accepts a String and an array and returns the index of the first occurrence in the String of any of the characters in the array (thus the name *index of any*). The documentation includes examples of what is returned for given inputs, as shown in Example 1-4.

Example 1-4. indexOfAny() example cases

```
StringUtils.indexOfAny("zzabyycdxx",['z','a']) == 0
StringUtils.indexOfAny("zzabyycdxx",['b','y']) == 3
StringUtils.indexOfAny("aba", ['z'])          == -1
```

As you can see in Example 1-4, the first occurrence of z or a within zzabyycdxx is at index 0, and the first occurrence of b or y is at position 3.

The essence of this problem can be stated as: for each of the searchChars, find the index of the first encountered match within the target string. The Scala implementation of this method, called firstIndexOfAny, is much more straightforward, as shown in Example 1-5.

Example 1-5. Scala version of firstIndexOfAny()

```
def firstIndexOfAny(input : String, searchChars : Seq[Char]) : Option[Int] = {
  def indexedInput = (0 until input.length).zip(input)
  val result = for (pair <- indexedInput;
                    char <- searchChars;
                    if (char == pair._2)) yield (pair._1)
  if (result.isEmpty)
    None
  else
    Some(result.head)
}
```

In Example 1-5, I create an indexed version of the input string. Scala's zip() method takes a collection (the range of numbers up to the length of my input string) and combines it with the collection of String characters, creating a new collection consisting of pairs from the original collection. For example, if my input string is zabycdxx, indexe dInput contains Vector ((0,z), (1,a), (2,b), (3,y), (4,c), (5,d), (6,x), (7,x)). The zip name comes from the result; it looks as if the two collections have been joined like the teeth of a zipper.

Once I have the indexed collection, I use Scala's for() comprehension to first look at the collection of search characters, then access each pair from the indexed collection. Scala allows shorthand access to collection elements, so I can compare the current search character to the second item for the collection (if (char == pair._2))). If the characters match, I return the index portion of the pair (pair._1).

A common source of confusion in Java is the presence of null: is it a legitimate return value or does it represent the absence of a value? In many functional langugages (Scala included), that ambiguity is avoided by the Option class, which contains either None, indicating no return, or Some, containing the returned values. For Example 1-5, the problems asks for only the first match, so I return result.head, the first element in the results collection.

The original mandate of the problem asked for the first match, but it is trivial to create a version that returns all matches. I can rewrite my example to return all the matches by changing the return type and eliminating the wrapper around the return value, as shown in Example 1-6.

Example 1-6. Returning a lazy list of matches

```
def indexOfAny(input : String, searchChars : Seq[Char]) : Seq[Int] = {
  def indexedInput = (0 until input.length).zip(input)
  for (pair <- indexedInput;
       char <- searchChars;
       if (char == pair._2)) yield (pair._1)
}
```

Rather than constrain the API, allow the consumer to decide how many values it needs. Running `firstIndexOfAny("zzabyycdxx", "by")` returns `3` whereas `indexOfAny("zzabyycdxx", "by")` returns `Vector(3, 4, 5)`.

CHAPTER 2

Shift

Learning a new programming language is easy: you merely learn the new syntax for familiar concepts. For example, if you decide to learn JavaScript, your first stop will be a resource that explains how JavaScript's if statement works. Typically, developers learn new languages by applying what they know about existing languages. But learning a new paradigm is difficult—you must learn to see different solutions to familiar problems.

Writing functional code doesn't require a shift to a functional programming language such as Scala or Clojure but rather a shift in the way you approach problems.

A Common Example

Once garbage collection became mainstream, it simultaneously eliminated entire categories of hard-to-debug problems and allowed the runtime to manage a process that is complex and error-prone for developers. Functional programming aims to do the same thing for the algorithms you write, allowing you to work at a higher level of abstraction while freeing the runtime to perform sophisticated optimizations. Developers receive the same benefits of lower complexity and higher performance that garbage collection provides, but at a more intimate level, in the way you devise solutions.

Imperative Processing

Imperative programming describes a style of programming modeled as a sequence of commands (imperatives) that modify state. A traditional for loop is an excellent example of the imperative style of programming: establish an initial state and execute a series of commands for each iteration of the loop.

To illustrate the difference between imperative and functional programming, I'll start with a common problem and its imperative solution. Let's say that you are given a list of names, some of which consist of a single character, and you are asked to return a comma-delimited string with the single letter names removed, with each name capitalized. Java code to implement this algorithm appears in Example 2-1.

Example 2-1. Typical company process (in Java)

```java
package com.nealford.functionalthinking.trans;

import java.util.List;

public class TheCompanyProcess {
    public String cleanNames(List<String> listOfNames) {
        StringBuilder result = new StringBuilder();
        for(int i = 0; i < listOfNames.size(); i++) {
            if (listOfNames.get(i).length() > 1) {
                result.append(capitalizeString(listOfNames.get(i))).append(",");
            }
        }
        return result.substring(0, result.length() - 1).toString();
    }

    public String capitalizeString(String s) {
        return s.substring(0, 1).toUpperCase() + s.substring(1, s.length());
    }
}
```

Because you must process the entire list, the easiest way to attack the problem in Example 2-1 is within an imperative loop. For each name, I check to see if its length is greater than the disallowed single character, then append the capitalized name onto result, along with a trailing comma. The last name in the final string shouldn't include the comma, so I strip it off the final return value.

Imperative programming encourages developers to perform operations within loops. In this case, I do three things: *filter* the list to eliminate single characters, *transform* the list to capitalize each name, then *convert* the list into a single string. For now, I'll call these three operations *Useful Things* to do to a list. In an imperative language, I must use the same low-level mechanism (iteration over the list) for all three types of processing. Functional languages offer specific helpers for these operations.

Functional Processing

Functional programming describes programs as expressions and transformations, modeling mathematical formulas, and tries to avoid mutable state. Functional programming languages categorize problems differently than imperative languages. The logical categories listed earlier (*filter*, *transform*, and *convert*) are represented as functions that implement the low-level transformation but rely on the developer to customize the low-level machinery with a higher-order function, supplied as one of the parameters. Thus, I could conceptualize the problem as the pseudocode in Example 2-2.

Example 2-2. Pseudocode for the "company process"

```
listOfEmps
    -> filter(x.length > 1)
    -> transform(x.capitalize)
    -> convert(x + "," + y)
```

Functional languages allow you to model this conceptual solution without worrying about the details.

Consider the company process example from Example 2-1 implemented in Scala, shown in Example 2-3.

Example 2-3. Processing functionally in Scala

```
val employees = List("neal", "s", "stu", "j", "rich", "bob", "aiden", "j", "ethan",
        "liam", "mason", "noah", "lucas", "jacob", "jayden", "jack")

val result = employees
  .filter(_.length() > 1)
  .map(_.capitalize)
  .reduce(_ + "," + _)
```

The use of Scala in Example 2-3 reads much like the pseudocode in Example 2-2, with necessary implementation details. Given the list of names, I first filter it, eliminating single characters. The output of that operation is then fed into the map function, which executes the supplied code block on each element of the collection, returning the transformed collection. Finally, the output collection from map flows to the reduce() function, which combines each element based on the rules supplied in the code block. In this case, to combine the first two elements, I concatenate them with a comma. In all three of these small functions, I don't care what the parameters are named, so Scala allows me to skip the names and use an underscore instead. In the case of reduce(), I still pass two parameters, which is the expected signature even though I'm using the same generic indicator, the underscore.

I chose Scala as the first language to show this implementation because of its somewhat familiar syntax and the fact that Scala uses industry-consistent names for these concepts. In fact, Java 8 has these same features, and closely resembles the Scala version, as shown in Example 2-4.

Example 2-4. Java 8 version of the Company Process

```
public String cleanNames(List<String> names) {
    if (names == null) return "";
    return names
            .stream()
            .filter(name -> name.length() > 1)
            .map(name -> capitalize(name))
            .collect(Collectors.joining(","));
```

```
    }

    private String capitalize(String e) {
        return e.substring(0, 1).toUpperCase() + e.substring(1, e.length());
    }
```

In Example 2-4, I use the `collect()` method rather than `reduce()` because it is more
efficient with the Java `String` class; `collect()` is a special case for `reduce()` in Java 8.
Otherwise, it reads remarkably similarly to the Scala code in Example 2-3.

If I was concerned that some of the items in the list might be `null`, I can easily add
another criterium to the stream:

```
return names
        .stream()
        .filter(name -> name != null)
        .filter(name -> name.length() > 1)
        .map(name -> capitalize(name))
        .collect(Collectors.joining(","));
```

The Java runtime is intelligent enough to combine the `null` check and length filter into
a single operation, allowing you to express the idea succinctly yet still have performant
code.

Groovy has these features but names them more consistently than scripting languages
such as Ruby. The Groovy version of the "company process" from Example 2-1 appears
in Example 2-5.

Example 2-5. Processing in Groovy

```
public static String cleanUpNames(listOfNames) {
    listOfNames
        .findAll { it.length() > 1 }
        .collect { it.capitalize() }
        .join ','
}
```

While Example 2-5 is structurally similar to the Scala code in Example 2-3, the method
names and substitution identifier differ. Groovy's `findAll` on a collection applies the
supplied code block and keeps the ones that yield `true`. Like Scala, Groovy allows developers to shortcut writing code blocks with single parameters; the Groovy substitution
mechanism is the implicit `it` keyword, which represents the single parameter. The
`collect` method, Groovy's version of `map`, executes the supplied code block on each
element of the collection. Groovy supplies a function (`join()`) that accepts a collection
of strings and concatenates them into a single string, using the supplied delimiter, which
is precisely what I need.

Clojure is a functional language and uses the more traditional function names, as shown
in Example 2-6.

Example 2-6. Processing in Clojure

```clojure
(defn process [list-of-emps]
  (reduce str (interpose ","
    (map s/capitalize (filter #(< 1 (count %)) list-of-emps)))))
```

Unless you are accustomed to reading Clojure, the structure of the code in Example 2-6 might be unclear. Lisps such as Clojure work "inside out," so the place to start is the final parameter value `list-of-emps`. Clojure's `(filter a b)` function accepts two parameters: a function to use for filtering (in this case, an anonymous function) and the collection to filter. You can write a formal function definition for the first parameter such as `(fn [x] (< 1 (count x)))`, but Clojure allows you to write anonymous functions more tersely as `#(< 1 (count %))`. As in the previous examples, the outcome of the filtering operation is a smaller collection.

The `(map a b)` function accepts the transformation function as the first parameter and the collection second, which in this case is the return value of the `(filter )` operation. `map`'s first parameter can be a custom function, but any function that accepts a single parameter will work, and the built-in `capitalize` function matches the requirement. Finally, the result of the `(map )` operation becomes the collection parameter for `(re duce )`, whose first parameter is the combination `(str )` function applied to the return of the `(interpose )` function, which inserts its first parameter between each element of the collection (except the last).

Even experienced developers suffer when functionality becomes too nested like this. Fortunately, Clojure includes macros that allow you to "unwind" structures like this into more readable order. Consider Example 2-7, which is functionally identical to the Example 2-6 version.

Example 2-7. Improved readability via the `thread-last` macro

```clojure
(defn process2 [list-of-emps]
  (->> list-of-emps
       (filter #(< 1 (count %)))
       (map s/capitalize)
       (interpose ",")
       (reduce str)))
```

The *thread-last* (`->>`) macro takes the very common operation of applying a variety of transformations on collections and reverses the typical Lisp ordering, restoring a more natural left-to-right reading. In Example 2-7, the collection (`list-of-emps`) appears first. Each subsequent form in the block is applied to the previous one. One of the strengths of Lisp lies in its syntactic flexibility: any time something becomes difficult to read, bend the syntax back toward readability.

All these languages include key concepts from functional programming. Part of transitioning to functional thinking is learning where to apply these higher-level abstractions and stop going immediately for detailed implementations.

What are the benefits of thinking at a higher level of abstraction? First, it encourages you to categorize problems differently, seeing commonalities. Second, it allows the runtime to be more intelligent about optimizations. In some cases, reordering the work stream makes it more efficient (for example, processing fewer items) if it doesn't change the ultimate outcome. Third, it allows solutions that aren't possible when the developer is elbow deep in the details of the engine. For example, consider the amount of work required to make the Java code in Example 2-1 run across multiple threads. Because you control the low-level details of iteration, you must weave the thread code into yours. In the Scala version, I can make the code parallel by adding `par` to the stream, as shown in Example 2-8.

Example 2-8. Scala processing in parallel

```
val parallelResult = employees
  .par
  .filter(_.length() > 1)
  .map(_.capitalize)
  .reduce(_ + "," + _)
```

I can make an almost identical change to the Java 8 version to achieve the same effect, as shown in Example 2-9.

Example 2-9. Java 8 parallel processing

```
public String cleanNamesP(List<String> names) {
    if (names == null) return "";
    return names
            .parallelStream()
            .filter(n -> n.length() > 1)
            .map(e -> capitalize(e))
            .collect(Collectors.joining(","));
}
```

Clojure has a similar drop-in replacement for common collection transformations that makes them seamlessly parallel. Working at a higher level of abstraction allows the runtime to optimize low-level details. Writing an industrial-strength virtual machine with garbage collection is an extraordinarily complex task, and developers gladly cede those responsibilities. JVM engineers improved developers' lives by mostly encapsulating garbage collection and eliminating it from daily consideration.

The same dual benefit exists for functional operations such as `map`, `reduce`, and `fil ter`. An excellent example is the Reducers Library (*http://bit.ly/reducers-library*) in Clojure. By making a library extension to the Clojure language, its creator Rich Hickey provided new versions of `vector` and `map` (as well as a new `fold` function that works with existing `vectors` and `maps`) that use the underlying Java Fork/Join library to provide parallel processing of collections. One of Clojure's selling points is that it removes concurrency as a developer concern just as Java removed garbage collection. The fact that Clojure developers use `map` instead of iteration means that they automatically receive upgraded abilities.

 Focus on results over steps.

Stop thinking about the low-level details of how iteration, transformation, and reduction work, and start noticing the prevalence of problems in those shapes.

As another example of transforming an imperative solution to a functional one, consider the problem of *perfect numbers* and number classification.

Case Study: Number Classification

The Greek mathematican Nicomachus devised a classification scheme for natural numbers, identifying each as belonging uniquely to the categories of *abundant*, *perfect*, or *deficient*. A perfect number equals the sum of its positive divisors—the pairs of numbers whose product yields the target number, excluding the number itself. For example, 6 is a perfect number because its divisors are 1, 2, 3, and 6 = 1 + 2 + 3; similarly, 28 is perfect because 28 = 1 + 2 + 4 + 7 + 14. The definition of perfect numbers delineates the classification scheme shown in Table 2-1.

Table 2-1. Integer classification scheme

Perfect	Sum of factors = number
Abundant	Sum of factors > number
Deficient	Sum of factors < number

One additional mathematics concept assists in the implementation: the *aliquot sum*, which is defined as the sum of the factors of a number not including the number itself, which is nominally one of the factors. Using an aliquot sum rather than the proper sum of the factors makes the comparisons for perfection easier: `aliquotSum == number` rather than `sum - number == number`.

Imperative Number Classification

For the implementation, I know that it's likely that several classifications will take place per number. Given these requirements, a Java solution appears in Example 2-10.

Example 2-10. Number classifier in Java

```java
import java.util.HashMap;
import java.util.HashSet;
import java.util.Map;
import java.util.Set;

public class ImpNumberClassifierSimple {
    private int _number;                        ❶
    private Map<Integer, Integer> _cache;       ❷

    public ImpNumberClassifierSimple(int targetNumber) {
      _number = targetNumber;
      _cache = new HashMap<>();
    }

    public boolean isFactor(int potential) {
      return _number % potential == 0;
    }

    public Set<Integer> getFactors() {
        Set<Integer> factors = new HashSet<>();
        factors.add(1);
        factors.add(_number);
        for (int i = 2; i < _number; i++)
            if (isFactor(i))
                factors.add(i);
        return factors;
    }

    public int aliquotSum() {                    ❸
        if (_cache.get(_number) == null) {
            int sum = 0;
            for (int i : getFactors())
                sum += i;
            _cache.put(_number, sum - _number);
        }
        return _cache.get(_number);
    }

    public boolean isPerfect() {
        return aliquotSum() == _number;
    }

    public boolean isAbundant() {
        return aliquotSum() > _number;
    }

    public boolean isDeficient() {
        return aliquotSum() < _number;
    }
}
```

❶   Internal state to hold the classification target number

❷   Internal cache to prevent recalcuating the sum unnecessarily

❸   Calculation of the `aliquotSum`, the sum of factors minus the number itself

In the `ImpNumberClassifierSimple` class in Example 2-10, two elements of internal state exist. The `number` field allows me to avoid passing it as a parameter to many functions. The `cache` holds a `Map`, used to cache the sums for each number, yielding faster results (lookup versus calculation) on subsequent invocations for a particular number. Internal state is common and encouraged in the object-oriented world because OOP languages utilitize encapsulation as one of their benefits. Separating state often makes engineering practices such as unit testing easier, allowing easy injection of values.

The code in Example 2-10 is finely factored, with many small methods. This is a side effect of test-driven development, but it also allows me to show each part of the algorithm. I'll gradually switch out some of the parts for more functional versions.

Slightly More Functional Number Classification

One of my goals when I wrote the code in Example 2-10 was testability. What if I additionally wanted to minimize shared state? To do so, I can eliminate the member variables and pass the needed values as parameters. Consider the updated version in Example 2-11.

Example 2-11. Slightly more functional number classifier

```java
import java.util.Collection;
import java.util.Collections;
import java.util.HashSet;
import java.util.Set;

public class NumberClassifier {

    public static boolean isFactor(final int candidate, final int number) {    ❶
        return number % candidate == 0;
    }

    public static Set<Integer> factors(final int number) {                      ❷
        Set<Integer> factors = new HashSet<>();
        factors.add(1);
        factors.add(number);
        for (int i = 2; i < number; i++)
            if (isFactor(i, number))
                factors.add(i);
        return factors;
    }

    public static int aliquotSum(final Collection<Integer> factors) {
        int sum = 0;
```

```
        int targetNumber = Collections.max(factors);
        for (int n : factors) {                                    ❸
            sum += n;
        }
        return sum - targetNumber;
    }

    public static boolean isPerfect(final int number) {
        return aliquotSum(factors(number)) == number;
    }
                                                                   ❹
    public static boolean isAbundant(final int number) {
        return aliquotSum(factors(number)) > number;
    }

    public static boolean isDeficient(final int number) {
        return aliquotSum(factors(number)) < number;
    }
}
```

❶ All methods must accept number as a parameter—no internal state exists to hold it.

❷ All methods are public static because they are *pure functions*, thus generically useful outside the number-classification realm.

❸ Note the use of the most general reasonable parameter, aiding reuse at the function level.

❹ The code is currently inefficient for repeating classifications; no caching.

In the slightly more functional NumberClassifier in Example 2-11, all the methods are really self-contained, *pure functions* (functions that have no side effects), with public, static scope. Because there is no internal state in this class, no reason exists to "hide" any of the methods. In fact, the factors method is potentially useful in many other applications, such as searching for prime numbers.

Typically, the finest-grained element of reuse in object-oriented systems is the class, and developers forget that reuse comes in smaller packages. For example, the sum method in Example 2-11 accepts a Collection<Integer> rather than a specific type of list. That interface is general for all collections of numbers, making it more generally reusable at the function level.

I also did not implement the caching scheme for sum in this solution. Keeping a cache implies persistent state, and I don't really have any place to hold that state in this version. The code in Example 2-11 is also less efficient compared to the same functionality in Example 2-10. Because no internal state exists to hold the sum, it must be recalculated each time. In a later version in Chapter 4, I preserve statefulness and regain the cache via *memoization*, but for now I've lost it.

Java 8 Number Classifier

The most dramatic addition to Java 8 are *lambda blocks*, its version of higher-order functions. With this simple addition, Java developers have access to some of the same high-level abstractions that traditional functional languages use.

Consider the Java 8 version of the number classfier, shown in Example 2-12.

Example 2-12. Number classifier in Java 8

```java
import java.util.List;
import java.util.stream.Collectors;
import java.util.stream.IntStream;
import java.util.stream.Stream;

import static java.lang.Math.sqrt;
import static java.util.stream.Collectors.toList;
import static java.util.stream.IntStream.range;

public class NumberClassifier {

    public static IntStream factorsOf(int number) {
        return range(1, number + 1)
                .filter(potential -> number % potential == 0);
    }

    public static int aliquotSum(int number) {
        return factorsOf(number).sum() - number;
    }

    public static boolean isPerfect(int number) {
        return aliquotSum(number) == number;
    }

    public static boolean isAbundant(int number) {
        return aliquotSum(number)> number;
    }

    public static boolean isDeficient(int number) {
        return aliquotSum(number) < number;
    }

}
```

The code in Example 2-12 is dramatically shorter and simpler than in the original imperative version (Example 2-10) or the slightly more functional version (Example 2-11). In Example 2-12, the factorsOf() method returns an IntStream, allowing me to chain other operations onto it, including a terminating one that causes the stream to generate values. In other words, the return from factorsOf() isn't a list of integers but rather a stream that hasn't generated any values yet. Writing the aliquotSum() method is trivial: it is the sum of the list of factors minus the number itself. In Example 2-12, I wasn't required to write the sum() method—in Java 8, it is one of the stream terminators that generates values.

In physics, energy is differentiated into *potential*, energy stored and ready to use, and *kinetic*, energy expenditure. For collections in languages such as Java before version 8, all collections acted as kinetic energy: the collection resolved values immediately, keeping no intermediate state. Streams in functional languages work more like potential energy, which is stored for later use. The stream holds the origin of the data (in Example 2-12, the origin comes from the range() method) and whatever criteria have been attached to the stream, such as filtering operations. The stream doesn't convert from potential to kinetic until the developer "asks" for values, using a terminating operation such as forEach() or sum(). The stream is passable as a parameter and can have additional criteria added later to its potential until it becomes kinetic. This is an example of *lazy evaluation*, which I cover in detail in Chapter 4.

This style of coding was possible, with difficulty, in previous versions of Java, using some useful frameworks.

Functional Java Number Classifier

While all modern languages now include higher-order functions, many organizations stay on older versions of runtimes such as Java for many years for nontechnical reasons. *Functional Java* is an open source framework whose mission includes adding as many functional idioms to Java post version 1.5 with as little intrusiveness as possible. For example, because the Java 1.5-era JDK don't include higher-order functions, Functional Java mimics their use via generics and anonymous inner classes. The number classifier takes on a different look when implemented using Functional Java's idioms, as shown in Example 2-13.

Example 2-13. Number classifier using the Functional Java framework

```
import fj.F;
import fj.data.List;
import static fj.data.List.range;

public class NumberClassifier {

    public List<Integer> factorsOf(final int number) {
        return range(1, number + 1)                         ❶
                .filter(new F<Integer, Boolean>() {
                    public Boolean f(final Integer i) {
                        return number % i == 0;
                    }
                });                                          ❷
    }

    public int aliquotSum(List<Integer> factors) {          ❸
        return factors.foldLeft(fj.function.Integers.add, 0) - factors.last();
```

```
        }

    public boolean isPerfect(int number) {
        return aliquotSum(factorsOf(number)) == number;
    }

    public boolean isAbundant(int number) {
        return aliquotSum(factorsOf(number)) > number;
    }

    public boolean isDeficient(int number) {
        return aliquotSum(factorsOf(number)) < number;
    }
}
```

❶   Ranges in Functional Java are noninclusive.

❷   Filter rather than iterate.

❸   Fold rather than iterate.

The primary differences between Examples 2-13 and 2-11 lie in two methods: `aliquot Sum()` and `factorsOf()`. The `aliquotSum()` method takes advantage of a method on the `List` class in Functional Java, the `foldLeft()` method. In this case, a "fold left" means:

1. Take an initial value (0 in this case) and combine it via an operation on the first element of the list.

2. Take the result and apply the same operation to the next element.

3. Keep doing this until the list is exhausted.

Notice that this is exactly what you do when you sum a list of numbers: start with zero, add the first element, take that result and add it to the second, and continue until the list is consumed. Functional Java supplies the higher-order function (in this example, the `Integers.add` function) and takes care of applying it for you. Of course, Java didn't have higher-order functions until Java 8. Functional Java uses anonymous inner classes to mimic the style if not the full capabilities of higher-order functions.

The other intriguing method in Example 2-13 is `factorsOf()`, which illustrates my "results over steps" mantra. What is the essence of the problem of discovering factors of a number? Stated another way, given a list of all possible numbers up to a target number, how do I determine which ones are factors of the number? This suggests a filtering operation—I can filter the entire list of numbers, eliminating those that don't meet my criteria. The method basically reads like this description: take the range of numbers from 1 to my number (the range is noninclusive, hence the incrementation by 1); filter the list based on the code in the `f()` method, which is Functional Java's way of allowing you to create a class with specific data types and return values.

In Example 2-13, I used the `foldLeft()` method, which collapses elements leftward, toward the first element. For addition, which is commutative, the direction doesn't matter. If, on the other hand, I need to use an operation in which order matters, there is also a `foldRight()` variant.

Higher-order abstractions eliminate friction.

You might think that the difference between the Functional Java version (Example 2-13) and the Java 8 version (Example 2-12) is merely syntactic sugar. (It is actually that plus more.) Yet syntactic convenience is important because *syntax* is the way you express ideas in a language.

I once had a memorable discussion with Martin Fowler in a taxicab in Barcelona, and we were talking about the waning of Smalltalk versus the waxing of Java. Fowler did extensive work in both and says that he initially viewed the switch from Smalltalk to Java as a syntactic inconvenience, but eventually as an impediment to the kinds of thinking afforded in the previous world. Placing syntactic hurdles around encouraged abstractions adds needless friction to the thought process.

Don't add needless friction.

Common Building Blocks

The categories of *Useful Things* I mentioned earlier appear in all the functional versions of the number classifier, with differing names. These *Useful Things* are ubiquitous in functional languages and frameworks.

Filter

A common operation on lists is filtering: creating a smaller list by filtering items in a list based on some user-defined criteria. Filtering is illustrated in Figure 2-1.

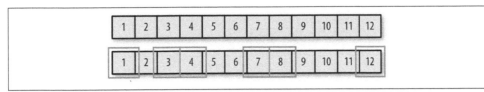

Figure 2-1. Filtering a list of numbers from a larger list

When filtering, you produce another list (or collection) potentially smaller than the original, depending on the filtering criteria. In the number-classifier example, I use filtering to determine the factors of a number, as shown in Example 2-14.

Example 2-14. Filtering in Java 8

```
public static IntStream factorsOf(int number) {
    return range(1, number + 1)
            .filter(potential -> number % potential == 0);
}
```

The code in Example 2-14 creates a range of numbers from 1 to the target number, then applies the `filter()` method to eliminate numbers that aren't factors of the target number: the Java modulus operator (%) returns the remainder from integer division, where a zero remainder indicates a factor.

Although it is possible to achieve the same results without lambda blocks (as in Example 2-13), it is more concise in a language with them. A Groovy version appears in Example 2-15.

Example 2-15. Using filtering (called findAll()) in Groovy

```
static def factors(number) {
  (1..number).findAll {number % it == 0}
}
```

In Example 2-15, rather than pass a single parameter, I use the single-parameter substitution keyword `it` as a placeholder, and the last line of the method is the method's return value, which is the list of factors in this case.

Use `filter` to produce a subset of a collection based on supplied filtering criteria.

Map

The *map* operation transforms a collection into a new collection by applying a function to each of the elements, as illustrated in Figure 2-2.

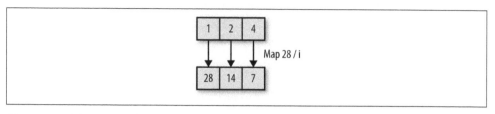

Figure 2-2. Mapping a function onto a collection

To illustrate `map()` and related transformations, I create an optimized version of my number classifier. First, I create an imperative version, shown in Example 2-16.

Example 2-16. Number classifier optimized

```java
import java.util.HashMap;
import java.util.HashSet;
import java.util.Map;
import java.util.Set;

import static java.lang.Math.sqrt;

public class ImpNumberClassifier {
    private int _number;                          ❶
    private Map<Integer, Integer> _cache;         ❷

    public ImpNumberClassifier(int targetNumber) {
        _number = targetNumber;
        _cache = new HashMap<>();
    }

    private boolean isFactor(int candidate) {
        return _number % candidate == 0;
    }

    private Set<Integer> getFactors() {
        Set<Integer> factors = new HashSet<>();
        factors.add(1);
        factors.add(_number);
        for (int i = 2; i <= sqrt(_number); i++)  ❸
            if (isFactor(i)) {
                factors.add(i);
                factors.add(_number / i);
            }
        return factors;
    }

    private int aliquotSum() {
        int sum = 0;
        for (int i : getFactors())
            sum += i;
```

```
        return sum - _number;
    }

    private int cachedAliquotSum() {                    ❹
        if (_cache.containsKey(_number))
            return _cache.get(_number);
        else {
            int sum = aliquotSum();
            _cache.put(_number, sum);
            return sum;
        }
    }

    public boolean isPerfect() {
        return cachedAliquotSum() == _number;
    }

    public boolean isAbundant() {
        return cachedAliquotSum() > _number;
    }

    public boolean isDeficient() {
        return cachedAliquotSum() < _number;
    }
}
```

❶   Internal state to prevent passing number as a parameter everywhere

❷   Internal cache for more efficient sum lookup

❸   A performance optimization is embedded in the getFactors() method. Observe that factors can always be harvested in pairs. For example, if the number in question is 16, when I grab the factor 2 I can also grab 8 because $2 \times 8 = 16$. If I harvest factors in pairs, I only need to check for factors up to the square root of the target number, which is precisely what the getFactors() method does.

❹   Method to return cached sum if possible

Groovy of course includes functional transformation functions; the Groovy version appears in Example 2-17, where Groovy's version of map() is called collect().

Example 2-17. Groovy optimized factors

```
static def factors(number) {
  def factors = (1..round(sqrt(number)+1)).findAll({number % it == 0})
  (factors + factors.collect {number / it}).unique()
}
```

In Example 2-17, the final call to unique() removes duplicates in the list, ensuring that whole-number square roots (such as 4) don't appear in the list twice. To see how far functional programming can transform your code, consider the version of the number classifier written in Clojure in Example 2-18.

Example 2-18. The (classify) function in Clojure encapsulates all the behavior within assignments

```
(defn classify [num]
  (let [factors (->> (range 1 (inc num))        ; ❶
                  (filter #(zero? (rem num %))))) ; ❷
        sum (reduce + factors)                    ; ❸
        aliquot-sum (- sum num)]                  ; ❹

    (cond                                         ; ❺
      (= aliquot-sum num) :perfect
      (> aliquot-sum num) :abundant
      (< aliquot-sum num) :deficient)))
```

❶ Methods become assignments.

❷ Assign factors to filtered range.

❸ Assign `sum` to reduced factors.

❹ Calculate aliquot sum.

❺ Return the keyword (enumeration) indicating the category.

If your functions collapse to single lines, you can shorten function definitions to a list of assigments, which is what happens in Example 2-18. The (`let` []) block in Clojure allows the creation of function-scoped assignments. First, I calculate the factors of the target number. To perform this calculation, I gather the range from 1 to the number ((`range 1 (inc num)`))—I call (`inc num`) because ranges in Clojure are noninclusive. Next, I use the (`filter`) method to eliminate unwanted factors. Usually, in Clojure, I write this expression as (`filter #(zero? (rem num %)) (range 1 (inc num)`)). However, because conceptually I generate the range first, I would rather it appear first as I read the code. Clojure's *thread-last* macro (the `->>` operator in Example 2-18) allows me to reorder it for readability. The assignment of `sum` and `aliquot-sum` are straightforward after I have the factors. The remaining body of the function compares the `aliquot-sum` in each case and returns the appropriate keyword (an enumeration delineated with a leading colon).

 Use *map* to transform collections in situ.

Fold/Reduce

The third common function has the most variations in name, and many subtle differences, among popular languages. foldLeft and reduce are specific variations on a list-manipulation concept called *catamorphism*, which is a generalization of list folding.

The reduce and fold operations have overlapping functionality, with subtle differences from language to language. Both use an *accumulator* to gather values. The reduce function is generally used when you need to supply an initial value for the accumulator, whereas fold starts with nothing in the accumulator. The order of operation on the collection is specified by the specific method name (for example, foldLeft or fold Right). Neither of these operations mutates the collection.

I show the foldLeft() function in Functional Java. In this case, a "fold left" means:

- Use a binary function or operator to combine the first element of the list, if any, with the initial value of an accumulator.
- Repeat step 1 until the list is exhausted and the accumulator holds the result of the fold.

Notice that this is exactly what you do when you sum a list of numbers: start with zero, add the first element, take that result and add it to the second, and continue until the list is consumed.

The aliquotSum() method in the Functional Java number classifier performs a sum across all the gathered factors and appears in Example 2-19.

Example 2-19. The foldLeft() method from Functional Java

```
public int aliquotSum(List<Integer> factors) {
    return factors.foldLeft(fj.function.Integers.add, 0) - factors.last();
}
```

At first it's not obvious how the one-line body in Example 2-19 performs a sum operation to calculate the aliquotSum. In this case, the *fold* operation refers to a transformation that combines each element of the list with the next one, accumulating a single result for the entire list. A fold left combines the list elements leftward, starting with a seed value and accumulating each element of the list in turn to yield a final result. Figure 2-3 illustrates a fold operation.

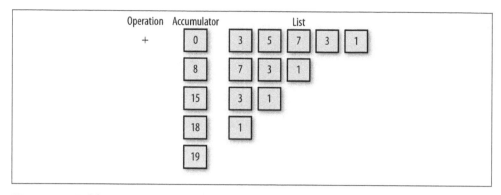

Figure 2-3. Fold operation

Because addition is commutative, it doesn't matter if you do a foldLeft() or fold Right(). But some operations (including subtraction and division) care about order, so the foldRight() method exists to handle those cases. In purely functional languages, left and right folds have implementation differences. For example, right folds can operate on infinite lists whereas left folds cannot.

Example 2-13 uses the Functional Java-supplied add enumeration; the framework includes the most common mathematical operations for you. But what about cases in which you need more refined criteria? Consider the code in Example 2-20.

Example 2-20. foldLeft() with user-supplied criteria

```
static public int addOnlyOddNumbersIn(List<Integer> numbers) {
    return numbers.foldLeft(new F2<Integer, Integer, Integer>() {
        public Integer f(Integer i1, Integer i2) {
            return (!(i2 % 2 == 0)) ? i1 + i2 : i1;
        }
    }, 0);
```

Functional Java is designed to work with pre-Java 8 JDKs, forcing the framework to improvise with single-method interfaces and anonymous inner classes. The built-in F2 class has the correct structure for a fold operation: it creates a method that accepts two integer parameters (these are the two values being folded upon one another) and the return type.

The reduce operation for Groovy's number classifier appears in Example 2-21.

Example 2-21. Groovy's version of reduce() (called inject())

```
static def sumFactors(number) {
    factors(number).inject(0, {i, j -> i + j})
}
```

Groovy's `inject` method uses the same signature of `reduce` shown in Example 2-18; the first parameter expects a seed value, and the second is a closure block that accepts two parameters and returns a single value. In this case, I add the two passed parameters: `{i, j → i + j}`.

Either `fold` or `reduce` is commonly used when you need to process a collection of items to produce a different-sized (usually smaller but not necessarily) value, which could be a collection or a single value.

 Use `reduce` or `fold` for piecewise collection processing.

Number classification is of course a contrived example, so it's hard to generalize to different types of problems. However, I've noticed a significant change in coding style on projects using languages that support these abstractions (whether they are functional languages or not). I first noticed this on Ruby on Rails projects. Ruby has these same list-manipulation methods that use closure blocks, and I was struck by how frequently `collect()`, `map()`, and `inject()` appear. Once you become accustomed to having these tools in your toolbox, you'll find yourself turning to them again and again.

One of the challenges of learning a different paradigm such as functional programming is learning the new building blocks and "seeing" them peek out of problems as a potential solution. In functional programming, you have far fewer abstractions, but each one is generic (with specificity added via higher-order functions). Because functional programming relies heavily on passed parameters and composition, you have fewer rules to learn about the interactions among moving parts, making your job easier.

Synonym Suffering

Functional programming languages feature several families of common functions. Yet developers sometimes have a hard time moving between languages because familiar functions have unfamiliar names. Functional languages tend to name these common functions based on functional paradigms. Languages that are derived from scripting backgrounds tend to use more descriptive names (sometimes multiple names, with several aliases that point to the same function).

Filter

With the filter function, you can specify a Boolean criterion (typically in the form of a higher-order function) to apply to a collection. The function returns the subset of the collection whose elements match the criterion. Filtering is closely related to find functions, which return the first matching element in a collection.

Scala

Scala has many filter variants. The simplest case filters a list based on passed criteria. In this first example, I create a list of numbers. Then I apply the `filter()` function, passing a code block that specifies the criterion that all elements must be divisible by 3:

```
val numbers = List.range(1, 11)
numbers filter (x => x % 3 == 0)
// List(3, 6, 9)
```

I can create a terser version of the code block by relying on implicit parameters:

```
numbers filter (_ % 3 == 0)
// List(3, 6, 9)
```

This second version is less verbose because Scala allows substitution of parameters with underscores. Both versions yield the same result.

Many examples of filtering operations use numbers, but `filter()` applies to any collection. This example applies `filter()` to a list of words to determine the three-letter words:

```
val words = List("the", "quick", "brown", "fox", "jumped",
                 "over", "the", "lazy", "dog")
words filter (_.length == 3)
// List(the, fox, the, dog)
```

Another filtering variant in Scala is the `partition()` function, which returns an alternate version of a collection by splitting it into multiple parts; the original collection is unchanged. The split is based on the higher-order function that you pass to determine the separation criteria. Here, the `partition()` function returns two lists that are split according to which list members are divisible by 3:

```
numbers partition (_ % 3 == 0)
// (List(3, 6, 9),List(1, 2, 4, 5, 7, 8, 10))
```

The `filter()` function returns a collection of matching elements, whereas `find()` returns only the first match:

```
numbers find (_ % 3 == 0)
// Some(3)
```

However, the return value for `find()` isn't the matched value itself, but rather one that's wrapped in an `Option` class. Option has two possible values: `Some` or `None`. Scala, like some other functional languages, uses `Option` as a convention to avoid returning `null` in the absence of a value. The `Some()` instance wraps the actual return value, which is 3 in the case of `numbers find (_ % 3 == 0)`. If I try to find something that doesn't exist, the return is `None`:

```
numbers find (_ < 0)
// None
```

I discuss `Option` and similar classes in depth in Chapter 5.

Scala also includes several functions that process a collection based on a predicate function and either retain values or discard them. The `takeWhile()` function returns the largest set of values from the front of the collection that satisfy the predicate function:

```
List(1, 2, 3, -4, 5, 6, 7, 8, 9, 10) takeWhile (_ > 0)
// List(1, 2, 3)
```

The `dropWhile()` function skips the largest number of elements that satisfy the predicate:

```
words dropWhile (_ startsWith "t")
// List(quick, brown, fox, jumped, over, the, lazy, dog)
```

Groovy

Groovy isn't considered a functional language, but it contains many functional paradigms—some with names that are derived from scripting languages. For example, the function that's traditionally called `filter()` in functional languages is Groovy's `findAll()` method:

```
(1..10).findAll {it % 3 == 0}
// [3, 6, 9]
```

Like Scala's filter functions, Groovy's work on all types, including strings:

```
def words = ["the", "quick", "brown", "fox", "jumped",
             "over", "the", "lazy", "dog"]
words.findAll {it.length() == 3}
// [The, fox, the, dog]
```

Groovy also has a `partition()`-like function called `split()`:

```
(1..10).split {it % 3}
// [ [1, 2, 4, 5, 7, 8, 10], [3, 6, 9] ]
```

The return value of the `split()` method is a nested array, like the nested list in Scala that's returned from `partition()`.

Groovy's `find()` method returns the first match from the collection:

```
(1..10).find {it % 3 == 0}
// 3
```

Unlike Scala, Groovy follows Java conventions and returns `null` when `find()` fails to find an element:

```
(1..10).find {it < 0}
// null
```

Groovy also has `takeWhile()` and `dropWhile()` methods with similar semantics to Scala's versions:

```
[1, 2, 3, -4, 5, 6, 7, 8, 9, 10].takeWhile {it > 0}
// [1, 2, 3]

words.dropWhile {it.startsWith("t")}
// [quick, brown, fox, jumped, over, the, lazy, dog]
```

As in the Scala example, `dropWhile()` acts as a specialized filter: it drops the largest prefix that matches the predicate, filtering only the first part of the list:

```
def moreWords = ["the", "two", "ton"] + words
moreWords.dropWhile {it.startsWith("t")}
// [quick, brown, fox, jumped, over, the, lazy, dog]
```

Clojure

Clojure has an astounding number of collection-manipulation routines, often usefully generic because of Clojure's dynamic typing. Many developers gravitate toward Clojure because of the richness and flexibility of its collection libraries. Clojure uses traditional functional programming names, as shown by the (`filter`) function:

```
(def numbers (range 1 11))
(filter (fn [x] (= 0 (rem x 3))) numbers)
; (3 6 9)
```

Like the other languages, Clojure has a terser syntax for simple anonymous functions:

```
(filter #(zero? (rem % 3)) numbers)
; (3 6 9)
```

And as in the other languages, Clojure's functions work on any applicable type, such as strings:

```
(def words ["the" "quick" "brown" "fox" "jumped" "over" "the" "lazy" "dog"])
(filter #(= 3 (count %)) words)
; (the fox the dog)
```

Clojure's return type for (`filter`) is a Seq, which is delineated by parentheses. The Seq interface is the core abstraction for sequential collections in Clojure.

Map

The second major functional transformation that's common to all functional languages is *map*. A map function accepts a higher-order function and a collection, then applies the passed function to each element and returns a collection. The returned collection (unlike with filtering) is the same size as the original collection, but with updated values.

Scala

Scala's `map()` function accepts a code block and returns the transformed collection:

```
List(1, 2, 3, 4, 5) map (_ + 1)
// List(2, 3, 4, 5, 6)
```

The `map()` function works on all applicable types, but it doesn't necessarily return a transformed version of each element of the collection. In this example, I return a list of the sizes of all elements in a string:

```
words map (_.length)
// List(3, 5, 5, 3, 6, 4, 3, 4, 3)
```

Nested lists occur so often in functional programming languages that library support for denesting—typically called *flattening*—is common. Here is an example of flattening a nested list:

```
List(List(1, 2, 3), List(4, 5, 6), List(7, 8, 9)) flatMap (_.toList)
// List(1, 2, 3, 4, 5, 6, 7, 8, 9)
```

The resulting `List` contains just the elements, with the extra infrastructure removed. The `flatMap()` function also works on data structures that might not seem nested in the traditional way. For example, you can consider a string as a series of nested characters:

```
words flatMap (_.toList)
// List(t, h, e, q, u, i, c, k, b, r, o, w, n, f, o, x, ...
```

Groovy

Groovy also includes several map variants called `collect()`. The default variant accepts a code block to apply to each element of the collection:

```
(1..5).collect {it += 1}
// [2, 3, 4, 5, 6]
```

Like the other languages, Groovy allows shorthand for simple anonymous higher-order functions; using the `it` reserved word for parameter substitution.

The `collect()` method works on any collection, as long as you can supply a reasonable predicate (a function that returns `true` or `false`). Thus, you can use `collect()` on a list of strings:

```
def words = ["the", "quick", "brown", "fox", "jumped",
                "over", "the", "lazy", "dog"]
words.collect {it.length()}
// [3, 5, 5, 3, 6, 4, 3, 4, 3]
```

Groovy also has a method similar to `flatMap()` that collapses inner structure, called `flatten()`:

```
[ [1, 2, 3], [4, 5, 6], [7, 8, 9] ].flatten()
// [1, 2, 3, 4, 5, 6, 7, 8, 9]
```

The `flatten()` method also works on nonobvious collections such as strings:

```
(words.collect {it.toList()}).flatten()
// [t, h, e, q, u, i, c, k, b, r, o, w, n, f, o, x, j, ...
```

Clojure

Clojure includes a (`map`) function that accepts a higher-order function (which includes operators) and a collection:

```
(map inc numbers)
; (2 3 4 5 6 7 8 9 10 11)
```

The first parameter for (`map`) can be any function that accepts a single parameter: a named function, an anonymous function, or a preexisting function such as `inc` that increments its argument. The more typical anonymous syntax is illustrated in this example, which generates a collection of the lengths of the words in a string:

```
(map #(count %) words)
; (3 5 5 3 6 4 3 4 3)
```

Clojure's (`flatten`) function is similar to Groovy's:

```
(flatten [[1 2 3] [4 5 6] [7 8 9]])
; (1 2 3 4 5 6 7 8 9)
```

Fold/Reduce

The third common function has the most variations in name, and many subtle differences.

Scala

Scala has the richest set of fold operations, in part because it facilitates several typing scenarios that don't appear in the dynamically typed Groovy and Clojure. Reduce is commonly used to perform sums:

```
List.range(1, 10) reduceLeft((a, b) => a + b)
// 45
```

The function that's supplied to `reduce()` is typically a function or operator that accepts two arguments and returns a single result, thereby consuming the list. You can use Scala's syntactic sugar to shorten the function definition:

```
List.range(1, 10).reduceLeft(0)(_ + _)
// 45
```

The reduceLeft() function assumes that the first element is the left side of the opera-tion. For operators such as plus, the placement of operands is irrelevant, but order matters for operations such as divide. If you want to reverse the order in which the operator is applied, use reduceRight():

```
List.range(1, 10) reduceRight(_ - _)

// 8 -    9  = -1
// 7 - (-1) = 8
// 6 -    8  = -2
// 5 - (-2) = 7
// 4 -    7  = -3
// 3 - (-3) = 6
// 2 -    6 = -4
// 1 - (-4) = 5
// result: 5
```

When I mentioned *reverse* above, the application may not be intiuitive. The reduce Right() function reduces the *direction* of operations but not the ordering of parameters. Thus, it applies 8 - 9 first, then uses that result as the *second* parameter in subsequent calculations.

Understanding when you can use higher-level abstractions such as reduce is one of the keys to mastery of functional programming. This example uses reduceLeft() to de-termine the longest word in a collection:

```
words.reduceLeft((a, b) => if (a.length > b.length) a else b)
// jumped
```

The reduce and fold operations have overlapping functionality, with subtle distinctions that I discussed earlier. One obvious difference suggests common uses. In Scala, the signature of reduceLeft[B >: A](op: (B, A) => B): B shows that the only parameter that's expected is the function to combine elements. The initial value is expected to be the first value in the collection. In contrast, the signature of foldLeft[B](z: B)(op: (B, A) => B): B indicates an initial seed value for the result, so you can return types that are different from the type of the list elements.

Here's an example of summing a collection by using foldLeft():

```
List.range(1, 10).foldLeft(0)(_ + _)
// 45
```

Scala supports operator overloading, so the two common fold operations, foldLeft and foldRight, have corresponding operators: /: and :\, respectively. Thus, you can create a terser version of sum by using foldLeft:

```
(0 /: List.range(1, 10)) (_ + _)
// 45
```

Similarly, to find the cascading difference between each member of a list (the reverse of a sum operation, admittedly a rare requirement) you can use either the `foldRight()` function or the `:\` operator:

```
(List.range(1, 10) :\ 0) (_ - _)
// 5
```

Groovy

Groovy's entry in the reduce category uses overloading of the `inject()` function to support the same functionality as Scala's `reduce()` and `foldLeft()` options. One version of the function accepts an initial value. This example uses the `inject()` method to generate a sum over a collection:

```
(1..10).inject {a, b -> a + b}
// 55
```

The alternate form accepts an initial value:

```
(1..10).inject(0, {a, b -> a + b})
// 55
```

Groovy has a much smaller functional library than Scala or Clojure—not surprising in view of the fact that Groovy is a multiparadigm language that doesn't emphasize functional programming.

Clojure

Clojure is primarily a functional programming language, so it supports (`reduce`). The (`reduce`) function accepts an optional initial value to cover both the `reduce()` and `foldLeft()` cases in Scala. The (`reduce`) function brings no surprises. It accepts a function that expects two arguments and a collection:

```
(reduce + (range 1 11))
; 55
```

Clojure includes advanced support for reduce-like functionality in a library called Reducers (*http://clojure.org/reducers*).

Part of the challenge of learning a different paradigm (such as functional programming) is learning new terminology. That effort is complicated when different communities use different terms. But once you grasp the similarities, you see that functional languages offer overlapping functionality in syntactically surprising ways.

CHAPTER 3

Cede

Confession: I never want to work in a non-garbage-collected language again. I paid my dues in languages like C++ for too many years, and I don't want to surrender the conveniences of modern languages. That's the story of how software development progresses. We build layers of abstraction to handle (and hide) mundane details. As the capabilities of computers have grown, we've offloaded more tasks to languages and runtimes. Developers used to shun interpreted languages as too slow, but they are now commonplace. Many of the features of functional languages were prohibitively slow a decade ago but make perfect sense now because they optimize developer time and effort.

One of the values of functional thinking is the ability to cede control of low-level details (such as garbage collection) to the runtime, eliminating a swath of bugs you must chase. While many developers are accustomed to blissful ignorance for bedrock abstractions such as memory, they are less accustomed to similar abstractions appearing at a higher level. Yet these higher-level abstractions serve the same purpose: handling the mundane details of machinery while freeing developers to work on unique aspects of their problems.

In this chapter, I show five ways developers in functional languages can cede control to the language or runtime, freeing themselves to work on more relevant problems.

Iteration to Higher-Order Functions

I already illustrated the first example of surrendering control in Example 2-3, replacing iteration with functions such as map. What's ceded here is clear: if you can express which operation you want to perform in a higher-order function, the language will apply it efficiently, including the ability to parallelize the operation with the addition of the par modifier.

Multithreaded code represents some of the most difficult and error-prone code to write and debug. Offloading the headache of thread management to a helper allows the developer to care less about the underlying plumbing.

That doesn't mean that developers should cede all responsibility for understanding what happens in lower-level abstractions. In many cases, you still must understand the implications of using abstractions such as Stream. For example, many developers were surprised that they still had to understand details of the Fork/Join library to achieve high performance, even with the new Stream API in Java 8. Once you understand it, however, you can apply that power in a more succinct way.

 Always understand one level below your normal abstraction layer.

Programmers rely on abstraction layers to be effective: no one programs a computer by manipulating bits of rust on hard drives using just 0 and 1. Abstractions hide messy details from us, but they sometimes hide important considerations as well. I discuss this issue in more depth in Chapter 8.

Closures

All functional languages include closures, yet this language feature is often discussed in almost mystical terms. A *closure* is a function that carries an implicit binding to all the variables referenced within it. In other words, the function (or method) encloses a context around the things it references.

Here is a simple example, written in Groovy, of creating a closure block with a binding, shown in Example 3-1.

Example 3-1. Simple closure binding in Groovy

```
class Employee {
  def name, salary
}

def paidMore(amount) {
  return {Employee e -> e.salary > amount}
}

isHighPaid = paidMore(100000)
```

In Example 3-1, I define a simple `Employee` class with two fields. Then, I define a `paidMore` function that accepts a parameter `amount`. The return of this function is a code block, or *closure*, accepting an `Employee` instance. The type declaration is optional but serves as useful documentation in this case. I can assign this code block to the name `isHighPaid`, supplying the parameter value of `100,000`. When I make this assignment, I *bind* the value of `100,000` to this code block forever. Thus, when I evaluate employees via this code block, it will opine about their salaries by using the permanently bound value, as shown in Example 3-2.

Example 3-2. Executing the closure block

```
def Smithers = new Employee(name:"Fred", salary:120000)
def Homer = new Employee(name:"Homer", salary:80000)
println isHighPaid(Smithers)
println isHighPaid(Homer)
// true, false
```

In Example 3-2, I create a couple of employees and determine if their salaries meet the criterion. When a closure is created, it creates an enclosure around the variables referenced within the scope of the code block (thus the name *closure*). Each instance of the closure block has unique values, even for private variables. For example, I can create another instance of my `paidMore` closure with another binding(and therefore another assignment), as shown in Example 3-3.

Example 3-3. Another closure binding

```
isHigherPaid = paidMore(200000)
println isHigherPaid(Smithers)
println isHigherPaid(Homer)
def Burns = new Employee(name:"Monty", salary:1000000)
println isHigherPaid(Burns)
// false, false, true
```

Closures are used quite often as a portable execution mechanism in functional languages and frameworks, passed to higher-order functions such as `map()` as the transformation code. Functional Java uses anonymous inner classes to mimic some of "real" closure behavior, but they can't go all the way because Java before version 8 didn't include closures. But what does that mean?

Example 3-4 shows an example of what makes closures so special.

Example 3-4. How closures work (in Groovy)

```
def Closure makeCounter() {
  def local_variable = 0
  return { return local_variable += 1 }  // ❶
}

c1 = makeCounter()      // ❷
c1()                    // ❸
c1()
c1()

c2 = makeCounter()      // ❹

println "C1 = ${c1()}, C2 = ${c2()}"
// output: C1 = 4, C2 = 1  // ❺
```

❶ The return value of the function is a code block, not a value.

❷ c1 now points to an instance of the code block.

❸ Calling c1 increments the internal variable; if I evaluated this expression, it would yield 1.

❹ c2 now points to a new, unique instance of makeCounter().

❺ Each instance has a unique instance of the internal state held in local_variable.

The makeCounter() function first defines a local variable with an appropriate name, then returns a code block that uses that variable. Notice that the return type for the makeCounter() function is Closure, not a value. That code block does nothing but increment the value of the local variable and return it. I've placed explicit return calls in this code, both of which are optional in Groovy, but the code is even more cryptic without them.

To exercise the makeCounter() function, I assign the code block to a variable named c1, then call it three times. I'm using Groovy's syntactic sugar to execute a code block (rather than the more verboase c1.call()), which is to place a set of parentheses adjacent to the code block's variable. Next, I call makeCounter() again, assigning a new instance of the code block to a variable c2. Last, I execute c1 again along with c2. Note that each of the code blocks has kept track of a separate instance of local_variable. The origin of the word *closure* hints to its operation via creating an *enclosing context*. Even though a local variable is defined within the function, the code block is bound to that variable because it references it, meaning that it must keep track of it while the code block instance is alive.

From an implementation standpoint, the closure instance holds onto an encapsulated copy of whatever is in scope when the closure is created, such as local_variable in

Example 3-4. When the closure block is garbage collected, all the references it owns are reclaimed as well.

It's a bad idea to create a closure just so that you can manipulate its interior state—it's done here to illustrate the inner workings of closure bindings. Binding constant or immutable values (as shown in Example 3-1) is more common.

The closest you could come to the same behavior in Java prior to Java 8, or in fact any language that has functions but not closures, appears in Example 3-5.

Example 3-5. makeCounter() in Java

```java
class Counter {
    public int varField;

    Counter(int var) {
        varField = var;
    }

    public static Counter makeCounter() {
        return new Counter(0);
    }

    public int execute() {
        return ++varField;
    }
}
```

Several variants of the Counter class are possible (creating anonymous versions, using generics, etc.), but you're still stuck with managing the state yourself. This illustrates why the use of closures exemplifies functional thinking: allow the runtime to manage state. Rather than forcing yourself to handle field creation and babying state (including the horrifying prospect of using your code in a multithreaded environment), cede that control and let the language or framework invisibly manage that state for you.

 Let the language manage state.

Closures are also an excellent example of *deferred execution*. By binding code to a closure block, you can wait until later to execute the block. This turns out to be useful in many scenarios. For example, the correct variables or functions might not be in scope at definition time but are at execution time. By wrapping the execution context in a closure, you can wait until the proper time to execute it.

Imperative languages use *state* to model programming, exemplified by parameter passing. Closures allow us to model *behavior* by encapsulating both code and context into a single construct, the closure, that can be passed around like traditional data structures and executed at exactly the correct time and place.

 Capture the *context*, not the *state*.

Currying and Partial Application

Currying and partial application are language techniques derived from mathematics (based on work by twentieth-century mathematician Haskell Curry and others). These techniques are present in various types of languages and are omnipresent in functional languages in one form or another. Both currying and partial application give you the ability to manipulate the number of arguments to functions or methods, typically by supplying one or more default values for some arguments (known as fixing arguments). Most functional languages include currying and partial application, but they implement them in different ways.

Definitions and Distinctions

To the casual observer, currying and partial application appear to have the same effect. With both, you can create a version of a function with presupplied values for some of the arguments:

- *Currying* describes the conversion of a multiargument function into a chain of single-argument functions. It describes the transformation process, not the invocation of the converted function. The caller can decide how many arguments to apply, thereby creating a derived function with that smaller number of arguments.

- *Partial application* describes the conversion of a multiargument function into one that accepts fewer arguments, with values for the elided arguments supplied in advance. The technique's name is apt: it partially applies some arguments to a function, returning a function with a signature that consists of the remaining arguments.

With both currying and partial application, you supply argument values and return a function that's invokable with the missing arguments. But currying a function returns the next function in the chain, whereas partial application binds argument values to values that you supply during the operation, producing a function with a smaller arity (number of arguments). This distinction becomes clearer when you consider functions with arity greater than two.

For example, the fully curried version of the process(x, y, z) function is process(x)(y)(z), where both process(x) and process(x)(y) are functions that accept a single argument. If you curry only the first argument, the return value of process(x) is a function that accepts a single argument that in turn accepts a single argument. In contrast, with partial application, you are left with a function of smaller arity. Using partial application for a single argument on process(x, y, z) yields a function that accept two arguments: process(y, z).

The two techniques' results are often the same, but the distinction is important and often misconstrued. To complicate matters further, Groovy implements both partial application and currying but calls both currying. And Scala has both partially applied functions and the PartialFunction class, which are distinct concepts despite the similar names.

In Groovy

Groovy implements currying through the curry() function, which originates from the Closure class.

Example 3-6. Currying in Groovy

```
def product = { x, y -> x * y }

def quadrate = product.curry(4)        ❶
def octate = product.curry(8)          ❷

println "4x4: ${quadrate.call(4)}"     ❸
println "8x5: ${octate(5)}"            ❹
```

❶ curry() fixes one parameter, returning a function that accepts a single parameter.

❷ The octate() function always multiples the passed parameter by 8.

❸ quadrate() is a function that accepts a single parameter and can be called via the call() method on the underlying Closure class.

❹ Groovy includes syntactic sugar, allowing you to call it more naturally as well.

In Example 3-6, I define product as a code block accepting two parameters. Using Groovy's built-in curry() method, I use product as the building block for two new code blocks: quadrate and octate. Groovy makes calling a code block easy: you can either explicitly execute the call() method or use the supplied language-level syntactic sugar of placing a set of parentheses containing any parameters after the code-block name (as in octate(5), for example).

Despite the name, curry() actually implements partial application by manipulating closure blocks underneath. However, you can simulate currying by using partial application to reduce a function to a series of partially applied single-argument functions, as shown in Example 3-7.

Example 3-7. Partial application versus currying in Groovy

```
def volume = {h, w, l -> h * w * l}
def area = volume.curry(1)
def lengthPA = volume.curry(1, 1)          ❶
def lengthC = volume.curry(1).curry(1)     ❷

println "The volume of the 2x3x4 rectangular solid is ${volume(2, 3, 4)}"
println "The area of the 3x4 rectangle is ${area(3, 4)}"
println "The length of the 6 line is ${lengthPA(6)}"
println "The length of the 6 line via curried function is ${lengthC(6)}"
```

❶ Partial application

❷ Currying

The volume code block in Example 3-7 computes the cubic volume of a rectangular solid using the well-known formula. I then create an area code block (which computes a rectangle's area) by fixing volume's first dimension (h, for height) as 1. To use volume as a building block for a code block that returns the length of a line segment, I can perform either partial application or currying. lengthPA uses partial application by fixing each of the first two parameters at 1. lengthC applies currying twice to yield the same result. The difference is subtle, and the end result is the same, but if you use the terms currying and partial application interchangeably within earshot of a functional programmer, count on being corrected. Unfortunately, Groovy conflates these two closely related concepts.

Functional programming gives you new, different building blocks to achieve the same goals that imperative languages accomplish with other mechanisms. The relationships among those building blocks are well thought out. *Composition* is a common combinatorial technique in functional languages, which I cover in detail in Chapter 6. Consider the Groovy code in Example 3-8.

Example 3-8. Composing functions in Groovy

```
def composite = { f, g, x -> return f(g(x)) }
def thirtyTwoer = composite.curry(quadrate, octate)

println "composition of curried functions yields ${thirtyTwoer(2)}"
```

In Example 3-8, I create a composite code block that composes two functions, or calls one function on the return of the other. Using that code block, I create a thirtyTwoer code block, using partial application to compose the two methods together.

In Clojure

Clojure includes the (`partial f a1 a2 …`) function, which takes a function f and a fewer-than-required number of arguments and returns a partially applied function that's invokable when you supply the remaining arguments. Example 3-9 shows two examples.

Example 3-9. Clojure's partial application

```
(def subtract-from-hundred (partial - 100))

(subtract-from-hundred 10)      ; same as (- 100 10)
; 90

(subtract-from-hundred 10 20)   ; same as (- 100 10 20)
; 70
```

In Example 3-9, I define a `subtract-from-hundred` function as the partially applied - operator (operators in Clojure are indistinguishable from functions) and supply `100` as the partially applied argument. Partial application in Clojure works for both single- and multiple-argument functions, as shown in the two examples in Example 3-9.

Because Clojure is dynamically typed and supports variable argument lists, currying isn't implemented as a language feature. Partial application handles the necessary cases. However, the namespace private (`defcurried …`) function that Clojure added to the Reducers library enables much easier definition of some functions within that library. Given the flexible nature of Clojure's Lisp heritage, it is trivial to widen the use of (`defcurried …`) to a broader scope if desired.

Scala

Scala supports currying and partial application, along with a trait that gives you the ability to define constrained functions.

Currying

In Scala, functions can define multiple argument lists as sets of parentheses. When you call a function with fewer than its defined number of arguments, the return is a function that takes the missing argument lists as its arguments. Consider the example from the Scala documentation that appears in Example 3-10.

Example 3-10. Scala's currying of arguments

```
def filter(xs: List[Int], p: Int => Boolean): List[Int] =
    if (xs.isEmpty) xs
    else if (p(xs.head)) xs.head :: filter(xs.tail, p)
    else filter(xs.tail, p)

def modN(n: Int)(x: Int) = ((x % n) == 0)
```

```
val nums = List(1, 2, 3, 4, 5, 6, 7, 8)
println(filter(nums, modN(2)))
println(filter(nums, modN(3)))
```

In Example 3-10, the `filter()` function recursively applies the passed filter criteria. The `modN()` function is defined with two argument lists. When I call `modN()` by using `filter()`, I pass a single argument. The `filter()` function accepts as its second argument a function with an `Int` argument and a `Boolean` return, which matches the signature of the curried function that I pass.

Partially applied functions

In Scala you can also partially apply functions, as shown in Example 3-11.

Example 3-11. Partially applying functions in Scala

```
def price(product : String) : Double =
  product match {
    case "apples" => 140
    case "oranges" => 223
}

def withTax(cost: Double, state: String) : Double =
  state match {
    case "NY" => cost * 2
    case "FL" => cost * 3
}


val locallyTaxed = withTax(_: Double, "NY")
val costOfApples = locallyTaxed(price("apples"))

assert(Math.round(costOfApples) == 280)
```

In Example 3-11, I first create a `price()` function that returns a mapping between product and price. Then I create a `withTax()` function that accepts cost and state as arguments. However, within a particular source file, I know that I will work exclusively with one state's taxes. Rather than "carry" the extra argument for every invocation, I partially apply the state argument and return a version of the function in which the state value is fixed. The `locallyTaxed()` function accepts a single argument, the cost.

Partial (constrained) functions

The Scala `PartialFunction` trait is designed to work seamlessly with pattern matching, which is covered in detail in Chapter 6. Despite the similarity in name, the `Partial Function` trait does not create a partially applied function. Instead, you can use it to define a function that works only for a defined subset of values and types.

Case blocks are one way to apply partial functions. Example 3-12 uses Scala's `case` without the traditional corresponding match operator.

Example 3-12. Using case *without* match

```
val cities = Map("Atlanta" -> "GA", "New York" -> "New York",
  "Chicago" -> "IL", "San Francsico " -> "CA", "Dallas" -> "TX")

cities map { case (k, v) => println(k + " -> " + v) }
```

In Example 3-12, I create a map of city and state correspondence. Then I invoke the `map()` function on the collection, and `map()` in turn pulls apart the key/value pairs to print them. In Scala, a code block that contains `case` statements is one way of defining an anonymous function. You can define anonymous functions more concisely without using `case`, but the `case` syntax provides the additional benefits that Example 3-13 illustrates.

Example 3-13. Differences between map *and* collect

```
List(1, 3, 5, "seven") map { case i: Int ? i + 1 } // won't work
// scala.MatchError: seven (of class java.lang.String)

List(1, 3, 5, "seven") collect { case i: Int ? i + 1 }
// verify
assert(List(2, 4, 6) == (List(1, 3, 5, "seven") collect { case i: Int ? i + 1 }))
```

In Example 3-13, I can't use `map` on a heterogeneous collection with `case`: I receive a `MatchError` as the function tries to increment the `"seven"` string. But `collect()` works correctly. Why the disparity and where did the error go?

Case blocks define partial functions, but not partially applied functions. *Partial functions* have a limited range of allowable values. For example, the mathematical function $1/x$ is invalid if $x = 0$.

Partial functions offer a way to define constraints for allowable values. In the `collect()` invocation in Example 3-13, the case is defined for `Int`, but not for `String`, so the `"seven"` string isn't collected.

To define a partial function, you can also use the `PartialFunction` trait, as illustrated in Example 3-14.

Example 3-14. Defining a partial function in Scala

```
val answerUnits = new PartialFunction[Int, Int] {
    def apply(d: Int) = 42 / d
    def isDefinedAt(d: Int) = d != 0
}

assert(answerUnits.isDefinedAt(42))
assert(! answerUnits.isDefinedAt(0))
```

```
assert(answerUnits(42) == 1)
//answerUnits(0)
//java.lang.ArithmeticException: / by zero
```

In Example 3-14, I derive answerUnits from the PartialFunction trait and supply two functions: apply() and isDefinedAt(). The apply() function calculates values. I use the isDefinedAt() method—required for a PartialFunction definition—to create constraints that determine arguments' suitability.

Because you can also implement partial functions with case blocks, answerUnits from Example 3-14 can be written more concisely, as shown in Example 3-15.

Example 3-15. Alternative definition for answerUnits

```
def pAnswerUnits: PartialFunction[Int, Int] =
    { case d: Int if d != 0 => 42 / d }

assert(pAnswerUnits(42) == 1)
//pAnswerUnits(0)
//scala.MatchError: 0 (of class java.lang.Integer)
```

In Example 3-15, I use case in conjunction with a guard condition to constrain values and supply results simultaneously. One notable difference from Example 3-14 is the MatchError (rather than ArithmeticException)—because Example 3-15 uses pattern matching.

Partial functions aren't limited to numeric types. You can use all types, including Any. Consider the implementation of an incrementer, shown in Example 3-16.

Example 3-16. Defining an incrementer in Scala

```
def inc: PartialFunction[Any, Int] =
    { case i: Int => i + 1 }

assert(inc(41) == 42)
//inc("Forty-one")
//scala.MatchError: Forty-one (of class java.lang.String)

assert(inc.isDefinedAt(41))
assert(! inc.isDefinedAt("Forty-one"))

assert(List(42) == (List(41, "cat") collect inc))
```

In Example 3-16, I define a partial function to accept any type of input (Any), but choose to react to a subset of types. However, notice that I can also call the isDefinedAt() function for the partial function. Implementers of the PartialFunction trait who use case can call isDefinedAt(), which is implicitly defined. Example 3-13 illustrated that map() and collect() behave differently. The behavior of partial functions explains the difference: `collect()` is designed to accept partial functions and to call the `isDefine dAt()` function for elements, ignoring those that don't match.

Partial functions and partially applied functions in Scala are similar in name, but they offer a different set of orthogonal features. For example, nothing prevents you from partially applying a partial function.

Common Uses

Despite the tricky definitions and myriad implementation details, currying and partial application do have a place in real-world programming.

Function factories

Currying (and partial application) work well for places where you implement a factory function in traditional object-oriented languages. To illustrate, Example 3-17 implements a simple adder function in Groovy.

Example 3-17. Adder and incrementer in Groovy

```
def adder = { x, y -> x + y}
def incrementer = adder.curry(1)

println "increment 7: ${incrementer(7)}" // 8
```

In Example 3-17, I use the `adder()` function to derive the incrementer function.

Template Method design pattern

One of the Gang of Four design patterns is the Template Method pattern. Its purpose is to help you define algorithmic shells that use internal abstract methods to enable later implementation flexibility. Partial application and currying can solve the same problem. Using partial application to supply known behavior and leaving the other arguments free for implementation specifics mimics the implementation of this object-oriented design pattern.

I show an example of using partial application and other functional techniques to deprecate several design patterns (including Template Method) in Chapter 6.

Implicit values

When you have a series of function calls with similar argument values, you can use currying to supply implicit values. For example, when you interact with a persistence framework, you must pass the data source as the first argument. By using partial application, you can supply the value implicitly, as shown in Example 3-18.

Example 3-18. Using partial application to supply implicit values

```
(defn db-connect [data-source query params]
    ...)

(def dbc (partial db-connect "db/some-data-source"))

(dbc "select * from %1" "cust")
```

In Example 3-18, I use the convenience dbc function to access the data functions without needing to provide the data source, which is supplied automatically. The essence of encapsulation in object-oriented programming—the idea of an implicit this context that appears as if by magic in every function—can be implemented by using currying to supply this to every function, making it invisible to consumers.

Recursion

Recursion, which (according to Wikipedia) is the "process of repeating items in a self-similar way," is another example of ceding details to the runtime, and is strongly associated with functional programming. In reality, it's a computer-sciencey way to iterate over things by calling the same method from itself, reducing the collection each time, and always carefully ensuring you have an exit condition. Many times, recursion leads to easy-to-understand code because the core of your problem is the need to do the same thing over and over to a diminishing list.

Seeing Lists Differently

Groovy significantly augments the Java collection libraries, including adding functional constructs. The first favor Groovy does for you is to provide a different perspective on lists, which seems trivial at first but offers some interesting benefits.

If your background is primarily in C or C-like languages (including Java), you probably conceptualize lists as indexed collections. This perspective makes it easy to iterate over a collection, even when you don't explicitly use the index, as shown in the Groovy code in Example 3-19.

Example 3-19. List traversal using (sometimes hidden) indexes

```
def numbers = [6, 28, 4, 9, 12, 4, 8, 8, 11, 45, 99, 2]

def iterateList(listOfNums) {
  listOfNums.each { n ->
    println "${n}"
  }
}
println "Iterate List"
iterateList(numbers)
```

Groovy also includes an eachWithIndex() iterator, which provides the index as a parameter to the code block for cases in which explicit access is necessary. Even though I don't use an index in the iterateList() method in Example 3-19, I still think of it as an ordered collection of slots, as shown in Figure 3-1.

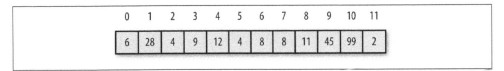

Figure 3-1. Lists as indexed slots

Many functional languages have a slightly different perspective on lists, and fortunately Groovy shares this perspective. Instead of thinking of a list as indexed slots, think of it as a combination of the first element in the list (the head) plus the remainder of the list (the tail), as shown in Figure 3-2.

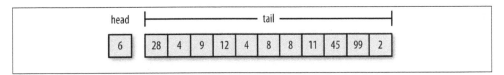

Figure 3-2. A list as its head and tail

Thinking about a list as head and tail allows me to iterate through it using recursion, as shown in Example 3-20.

Example 3-20. List traversal using recursion

```
def recurseList(listOfNums) {
  if (listOfNums.size == 0) return;
    println "${listOfNums.head()}"
    recurseList(listOfNums.tail())
}
println "\nRecurse List"
recurseList(numbers)
```

In the recurseList() method in Example 3-20, I first check to see if the list that's passed as the parameter has no elements in it. If that's the case, then I'm done and can return. If not, I print out the first element in the list, available via Groovy's head() method, and then recursively call the recurseList() method on the remainder of the list.

Recursion often has technical limits built into the platform, so this technique isn't a panacea. But it should be safe for lists that contain a small number of items.

I'm more interested in investigating the impact on the structure of the code, in antici-
pation of the day when the limits ease or disappear, as they always do as languages *evolve*
(see Chapter 5). Given the shortcomings, the benefit of the recursive version might not
be immediately obvious. To make it more so, consider the problem of filtering a list. In
Example 3-21, I show a filtering method that accepts a list and a predicate (a Boolean
test) to determine if the item belongs in the list.

Example 3-21. Imperative filtering with Groovy

```
def filter(list, predicate) {
  def new_list = []
  list.each {
    if (predicate(it)) {
      new_list << it
    }
  }
  return new_list
}

modBy2 = { n -> n % 2 == 0}

l = filter(1..20, modBy2)
println l
```

The code in Example 3-21 is straightforward: I create a holder variable for the elements
that I want to keep, iterate over the list, check each element with the inclusion predicate,
and return the list of filtered items. When I call `filter()`, I supply a code block specifying the filtering criteria.

Consider a recursive implementation of the filter method from Example 3-21, shown
in Example 3-22.

Example 3-22. Recursive filtering with Groovy

```
def filterR(list, pred) {
  if (list.size() == 0) return list
  if (pred(list.head()))
    [] + list.head() + filterR(list.tail(), pred)
  else
    filterR(list.tail(), pred)
}

println "Recursive Filtering"
println filterR(1..20, {it % 2 == 0})
//// [2, 4, 6, 8, 10, 12, 14, 16, 18, 20]
```

In the `filter()` method in Example 3-22, I first check the size of the passed list and
return it if it has no elements. Otherwise, I check the head of the list against my filtering
predicate; if it passes, I add it to the list (with an initial empty list to make sure that I
always return the correct type); otherwise, I recursively filter the tail.

The difference between Examples 3-21 and 3-22 highlights an important question: Who's minding the state? In the imperative version, *I* am. *I* must create a new variable named new_list, *I* must add things to it, and *I* must return it when I'm done. In the recursive version, the *language* manages the return value, building it up on the stack as the recursive return for each method invocation. Notice that every exit route of the filter() method in Example 3-22 is a return call, which builds up the intermediate value on the stack. You can cede responsibility for new_list; the language is managing it for you.

 Recursion allows you to cede state management to the runtime.

The same filtering technique illustrated in Example 3-22 is a natural fit for a functional language such as Scala, which combines currying and recursion, shown in Example 3-23.

Example 3-23. Recursive filtering in Scala

```scala
object CurryTest extends App {

  def filter(xs: List[Int], p: Int => Boolean): List[Int] =
    if (xs.isEmpty) xs
    else if (p(xs.head)) xs.head :: filter(xs.tail, p)
    else filter(xs.tail, p)

  def dividesBy(n: Int)(x: Int) = ((x % n) == 0) // ❶

  val nums = List(1, 2, 3, 4, 5, 6, 7, 8)
  println(filter(nums, dividesBy(2)))  // ❷
  println(filter(nums, dividesBy(3)))
}
```

❶ Function is defined to be curried.

❷ filter expects as parameters a collection (nums) and a function that accepts a single parameter (the curried dividesBy() function).

The list-construction operators in Scala make the return conditions for both cases quite readable and easy to understand. The code in Example 3-23 is one of the examples of both recursion and currying from the Scala documentation. The filter() method recursively filters a list of integers via the parameter p, a predicate function—a common term in the functional world for a Boolean function. The filter() method checks to see if the list is empty and, if it is, simply returns; otherwise, it checks the first element in the list (xs.head) via the predicate to see if it should be included in the filtered list.

If it passes the predicate condition, the return is a new list with the head at the front and the filtered tail as the remainder. If the first element fails the predicate test, the return becomes solely the filtered remainder of the list.

Although not as dramatic a life improvement as garbage collection, recursion does illustrate an important trend in programming languages: offloading moving parts by ceding it to the runtime. If I'm never allowed to touch the intermediate results of the list, I cannot introduce bugs in the way that I interact with it.

Tail-Call Optimization

One of the major reasons that recursion isn't a more commonplace operation is stack growth. Recursion is generally implemented to place intermediate results on the stack, and languages not optimized for recursion will suffer stack overflow. Languages such as Scala and Clojure have worked around this limitation in various ways. One particular way that developers can help runtimes handle this problem is *tail-call optimization*. When the recursive call is the last call in the function, runtimes can often replace the results on the stack rather than force it to grow.

Many functional languages (such as Erlang (*http://erlang.org*)), implement tail recursion without stack growth. Tail recursion is used to implement long-running Erlang processes that act as microservices within the application, receiving messages from other processes and carrying out tasks on their behalf as directed by those messages. The tail-recursive loop receiving and acting on messages also allows for the maintenance of state internal to the microservice, because any effects on the current state, which is immutable, can be reflected by passing a new state variable to the next recursion. Given Erlang's impressive fault-tolerance capabilities, there are likely tail-recursive loops in production that have run for years uninterrupted.

My guess is that you don't use recursion at all now—it's not even a part of your tool box. However, part of the reason lies in the fact that most imperative languages have lackluster support for it, making it more difficult to use than it should be. By adding clean syntax and support, functional languages make recursion a candidate for simple code reuse.

Streams and Work Reordering

One of the advantages of switching from an imperative to a functional style lies in the runtime's ability to make efficiency decisions for you.

Consider the Java 8 version of the "company process" from Chapter 2, repeated in Example 3-24 with a slight difference.

Example 3-24. Java 8 version of the company process

```
public String cleanNames(List<String> names) {
    if (names == null) return "";
    return names
            .stream()
            .map(e -> capitalize(e))
            .filter(n -> n.length() > 1)
            .collect(Collectors.joining(","));
}
```

Astute readers will notice that I changed the order of operations in this version of cleanNames() (in contrast to Example 2-4 in Chapter 2), putting the map() operation before filter(). When thinking imperatively, the instinct is to place the filtering operation before the mapping operation, so that the map has less work to perform, filtering a smaller list. However, many functional languages (including Java 8 and even the Functional Java framework) define a Stream abstraction. A Stream acts in many ways like a collection, but it has no backing values, and instead uses a stream of values from a source to a destination. In Example 3-24, the source is the names collection and the destination (or "terminal") is collect(). Between these operations, both map() and filter() are *lazy*, meaning that they defer execution as long as possible. In fact, they don't try to produce results until a downstream terminal "asks" for them.

For the lazy operations, intelligent runtimes can reorder the result of the operation for you. In Example 3-24, the runtime can flip the order of the lazy operations to make it more efficient, performing the filtering before the mapping. As with many functional additions to Java, you must ensure that the lambda blocks you pass to functions such as filter() don't have side effects, which will lead to unpredictable results.

Allowing the runtime to optimize when it can is another great example of ceding control: giving away mundane details and focusing on the problem domain rather than the *implementation* of the problem domain.

I discuss laziness in more detail in Chapter 4 and Java 8 streams in Chapter 7.

Smarter, Not Harder

Switching paradigms yields benefits, allowing you to get more work done with less effort. Many functional programming constructs do just that: remove annoying implementation details for common problems.

In this chapter, I discuss two features common in functional languages: *memoization* and *laziness*.

Memoization

The word memoization was coined by Donald Michie, a British artificial-intelligence researcher, to refer to function-level caching for repeating values. Today, memoization is common in functional programming languages, either as a built-in feature or one that's relatively easy to implement.

Memoization helps in the following scenario. Suppose you have a performance-intensive function that you must call repeatedly. A common solution is to build an internal cache. Each time you calculate the value for a certain set of parameters, you put that value in the cache, keyed to the parameter value(s). In the future, if the function is invoked with previous parameters, return the value from the cache rather than recalculate it. Function caching is a classic computer science trade-off: it uses more memory (which we frequently have in abundance) to achieve better performance over time.

Functions must be *pure* for the caching technique to work. A *pure* function is one that has no side effects: it references no other mutable class fields, doesn't set any values other than the return value, and relies only on the parameters for input. All the methods in the java.lang.Math class are excellent examples of pure functions. Obviously, you can reuse cached results successfully only if the function reliably returns the same values for a given set of parameters.

Caching

Caching is a common requirement (and source of hard-to-find bugs). In this section, I investigate two caching use cases for functions: intraclass versus external calls. I also illustrate two alternatives for implementing caching: hand-crafted state and memoization.

Method-level caching

In previous chapters, I've used the number classification problem as a canvas for solutions. The Classifier class classifies numbers, and a common use for it would entail running the same number through multiple methods for classification. For example, consider this code:

```
if (Classifier.isPerfect(n)) print "!"
else if (Classifier.isAbundant(n)) print "+"
else if (Classifier.isDeficient(n)) print "-"
```

In the previous implementations, I must recalculate the sum of the factors for every classification method that I call. This is an example of *intraclass caching*: during normal use, the sumOfFactors() method is typically called multiple times per number. In this common use case, this is an inefficient approach.

Caching sum

One of the ways to make the code more efficient is to leverage hard work already done. Because generating the sum of the factors is expensive, I want to do it only once for each number. Toward that end, I create a cache to store calculations, as shown in Example 4-1.

Example 4-1. Caching sum

```
class ClassifierCachedSum {
  private sumCache = [:]

  def sumOfFactors(number) {
    if (! sumCache.containsKey(number)) {
      sumCache[number] = factorsOf(number).sum()
    }
    return sumCache[number]

  }
}
// remainder of code unchanged...
```

In Example 4-1, I create a hash named sumCache as part of the class initialization. In the sumOfFactors() method, I check to see if the sum for the parameter is already cached and return it. Otherwise, I do the expensive calculation and put the sum in the cache before returning it.

The code is more complicated, but the results speak for themselves. I run all the examples through a series of unit tests that follow the pattern shown in Example 4-2.

Example 4-2. Testing nonoptimized speed

```
def static final TEST_NUMBER_MAX = 5000

@Test
void mashup() {
  println "Test for range 1-${TEST_NUMBER_MAX}"
  print "Non-optimized:           "
  start = System.currentTimeMillis()
  (1..TEST_NUMBER_MAX).each {n ->
    if (Classifier.isPerfect(n)) print '!'
    else if (Classifier.isAbundant(n)) print '+'
    else if (Classifier.isDeficient(n)) print '-'
  }
  println "\n\t ${System.currentTimeMillis() - start} ms"
  print "Non-optimized (2nd):        "
  start = System.currentTimeMillis()
  (1..TEST_NUMBER_MAX).each {n ->
    if (Classifier.isPerfect(n)) print '!'
    else if (Classifier.isAbundant(n)) print '+'
    else if (Classifier.isDeficient(n)) print '-'
  }
  println "\n\t ${System.currentTimeMillis() - start} ms"
```

When I run the tests in Example 4-2, the results in Table 4-1 indicate that the caching helps.

Table 4-1. Results for range 1–1,000

Version	Results (smaller is better)
Nonoptimized	577 ms
Nonoptimized (2nd)	280 ms
Cached sum	600 ms
Cached sum (2nd)	50 ms

The output illustrates that the nonoptimized version runs in 577 ms the first time, compared to the cached version, which takes 600 ms for its first run. For these two cases, the difference is insignificant, and you can see the slight overhead to build the cache. However, the second run of the nonoptimized version scores 280 ms. The difference between the first and second can be attributed to environmental factors such as garbage collection. The second run of the cached version shows a dramatic speed increase, scoring a mere 50 ms. When the second run happens, all the values are cached; now I'm measuring how fast I can read from a hash. The difference between the nonoptimized first run and the cached first run is negligible, but it's dramatic for the second run. This is an example of *external caching*: the overall results are used by whoever is calling the code, so the second run is very fast.

Caching sums makes a huge difference but includes trade-offs. `ClassifierCachedSum` can no longer contain pure static methods. The internal cache represents state, so I must make all the methods that interact with the cache nonstatic, which has a ripple effect. I could rig some `Singleton` solution, but that adds complexity too and a raft of testing issues. Because I control the cache variable, I must ensure correctness (by using tests, for example). Although caching improves performance, it isn't free: it adds accidental complexity and a maintenance burden to my code.

Caching everything

If caching the sums speeds up the code so much, why not cache every intermediate result that's likely to recur? That's the goal in Example 4-3.

Example 4-3. Caching everything

```
class ClassifierCached {
  private sumCache = [:], factorCache = [:]

  def sumOfFactors(number) {
    if (! sumCache.containsKey(number))
      sumCache[number] = factorsOf(number).sum()
    sumCache[number]
  }

  def isFactor(number, potential) {
    number % potential == 0;
  }

  def factorsOf(number) {
    if (! factorCache.containsKey(number))
      factorCache[number] = (1..number).findAll {isFactor(number, it)}
    factorCache[number]
  }

  def isPerfect(number) {
    sumOfFactors(number) == 2 * number
  }

  def isAbundant(number) {
    sumOfFactors(number) > 2 * number
  }

  def isDeficient(number) {
    sumOfFactors(number) < 2 * number
  }

}
```

In `ClassifierCached` in Example 4-3, I add caches both for the sum of factors and for the factors of a number—the increased performance appears in the test run results in Table 4-2.

Table 4-2. Results for range 1–1,000

Version	Results (smaller is better)
Nonoptimized	577 ms
Nonoptimized (2nd)	280 ms
Cached sum	600 ms
Cached sum (2nd)	50 ms
Cached	411 ms
Cached (2nd)	38 ms

The fully cached version (which is an entirely new class and instance variable in these test runs) scores 411 ms for the first run and a blazing 38 ms in the second run, once the cache has been primed. Although these results are good, this approach doesn't scale particularly well. In this test run, which shows results for testing 8,000 numbers, the outcome is more dire:

```
java.lang.OutOfMemoryError: Java heap space
        at java.util.ArrayList.<init>(ArrayList.java:112)
...more bad things...
```

As these results show, the developer responsible for the caching code must worry about both its correctness and its execution conditions. This is a perfect example of moving parts: state in code that a developer must maintain and dissect implications for. Many languages have advanced beyond this constraint, using mechanisms like *memoization*.

Adding Memoization

Functional programming strives to minimize moving parts by building reusable mechanisms into the runtime. Memoization is a feature built into a programming language that enables automatic caching of recurring function-return values. In other words, it automatically supplies the code I've written in Examples 4-1 and 4-3. Many modern languages support memoization, including Groovy.

In order to memoize a function in Groovy, you define it as a closure, then execute the `memoize()` method to return a function whose results will be cached.

Memoizing a function is a *metafunction* application: doing something to the function itself rather than the function results. Currying, discussed in Chapter 3, is another example of a metafunction technique. Groovy built memoization into its `Closure` class; other languages implement it differently.

To implement caching for sumOfFactors() as I did in Example 4-1, I memoize the sumOfFactors() method, as shown in Example 4-4.

Example 4-4. Memoizing sum

```
package com.nealford.ft.memoization

class ClassifierMemoizedSum {
  def static isFactor(number, potential) {
    number % potential == 0;
  }

  def static factorsOf(number) {
    (1..number).findAll { i -> isFactor(number, i) }
  }

  def static sumFactors = { number ->
    factorsOf(number).inject(0, {i, j -> i + j})
  }
  def static sumOfFactors = sumFactors.memoize()

  def static isPerfect(number) {
    sumOfFactors(number) == 2 * number
  }

  def static isAbundant(number) {
    sumOfFactors(number) > 2 * number
  }

  def static isDeficient(number) {
    sumOfFactors(number) < 2 * number
  }
}
```

In Example 4-4, I create the sumFactors() method as a code block (note the = and parameter placement). This is a pretty generic method and could just as well be pulled from a library somewhere. To memoize it, I assign the name sumOfFactors as the memoize() method call on the function reference.

Running the memoized version yields the results shown in Table 4-3.

Table 4-3. Results for range 1–1,000

Version	Results (smaller is better)
Nonoptimized	577 ms
Nonoptimized (2nd)	280 ms
Cached sum	600 ms
Cached sum (2nd)	50 ms
Cached	411 ms
Cached (2nd)	38 ms
Partially memoized	228 ms
Partially memoized (2nd)	60 ms

The partially memoized second run shows the same dramatic speed increase as the handwritten cached-sum version—with literally a two-line change to the original code (changing `sumFactors()` into a code block, and making `sumOfFactors()` point to a memoized instance of the code block).

Just as I cached everything earlier, why not memoize everything with potentially reusable results? That version of the classifier appears in Example 4-5, with the results shown in Table 4-4.

Example 4-5. Memoizing everything

```
package com.nealford.ft.memoization

class ClassifierMemoized {
  def static dividesBy = { number, potential ->
    number % potential == 0
  }
  def static isFactor = dividesBy.memoize()

  def static factorsOf(number) {
    (1..number).findAll { i -> isFactor.call(number, i) }
  }

  def static sumFactors = { number ->
    factorsOf(number).inject(0, {i, j -> i + j})
  }
  def static sumOfFactors = sumFactors.memoize()

  def static isPerfect(number) {
    sumOfFactors(number) == 2 * number
  }

  def static isAbundant(number) {
    sumOfFactors(number) > 2 * number
  }
```

```
def static isDeficient(number) {
    sumOfFactors(number) < 2 * number
  }
}
```

Table 4-4. Results for range 1–1,000

Version	Results (smaller is better)
Nonoptimized	577 ms
Nonoptimized (2nd)	280 ms
Cached sum	600 ms
Cached sum (2nd)	50 ms
Cached	411 ms
Cached (2nd)	38 ms
Partially memoized	228 ms
Partially memoized (2nd)	60 ms
Memoized	956 ms
Memoized (2nd)	19 ms

Memoizing everything slows down the first run but has the fastest subsequent run of any case—but only for small sets of numbers. As with the imperative caching solution tested in Example 4-3, large number sets impede performance drastically. In fact, the memoized version runs out of memory in the 8,000-number case. But for the imperative approach to be robust, safeguards and careful awareness of the execution context are required—another example of imperative moving parts. With memoization, optimization occurs at the function level. Look at the memoization results for 10,000 numbers found in Table 4-5.

Table 4-5. Results for range 1–10,000

Version	Results (smaller is better)
Nonoptimized	41,909 ms
Nonoptimized (2nd)	22,398 ms
Memoize at most 1000	55,685 ms
Memoize at most 1000 (2nd)	98 ms

I produced the results in Table 4-5 by calling the `memoizeAtMost(1000)` method instead of `memoize()`. Like other languages that support memoization, Groovy has several methods to help optimize results, as shown in Table 4-6.

Table 4-6. Memoization methods in Groovy

Method	Description
memoize()	Creates a caching variant of the closure
memoizeAtMost()	Creates a caching variant of the closure with an upper limit on the cache size
memoizeAtLeast()	Creates a caching variant of the closure with automatic cache size adjustment and lower limit on the cache size
memoizeBetween()	Creates a caching variant of the closure with automatic cache size adjustment and lower and upper limits on the cache size

In the imperative version, the developer owns the code (and responsibility). Functional languages build generic machinery—sometimes with customization knobs (in the form of alternate functions or parameters)—that you can apply to standard constructs. Functions are a fundamental language element, so optimizing at that level gives you advanced functionality for free. The memoization versions in this chapter with small number sets outperform the handwritten caching code handily. In fact, I'll never be able to create a cache as efficient as the language designers can because they can bend their own rules: language designers have access to low-level parts that developers don't, providing optimization opportunities beyond the grasp of mere mortals. Not only can the language handle caching more efficiently, I want to cede that responsibility to the runtime so I can think about problems at a higher level of abstraction.

 Language designers will always build more efficient mechanisms because they are allowed to bend rules.

Building a cache by hand is straightforward, but it adds statefulness and complexity to the code. Using functional-language features like memoization, I can add caching at the function level, achieving better results (with virtually no change to my code) than the imperative version. Functional programming eliminates moving parts, allowing you to focus your energy on solving real problems.

Of course, you don't have to rely on an existing class to layer memoization atop it. The memoize() family of functions is implemented as part of the Closure library class. Consider the example of inline memoization declaration shown in Example 4-6.

Example 4-6. Inline memoization in Groovy

```
package com.nealford.javanext.memoizehashing

class NameHash {
  def static hash = {name ->
    name.collect{rot13(it)}.join()
  }.memoize()
```

```
public static char rot13(s) {
  char c = s
  switch (c) {
    case 'A'..'M':
    case 'a'..'m': return c + 13
    case 'N'..'Z':
    case 'n'..'z': return c - 13
    default: return c
  }
}

}
```

I don't mean to suggest that the rot13() algorithm (a version of the Caesar Cipher) in Example 4-6 is performance challenged, so just pretend that it is worth caching. Note the slightly unusual function-definition syntax in the assignment of the code block to the hash variable. The last part of the definition is the call to memoize(), meaning that a nonmemoized version doesn't exist in this case.

A unit test that calls the memoized function appears in Example 4-7.

Example 4-7. Testing memoized hashing function

```
class NameHashTest extends GroovyTestCase {
  void testHash() {
    assertEquals("ubzre", NameHash.hash.call("homer"))  }
}
```

In Example 4-7, I must call the memoized function with an extra call() invocation. Generally, in Groovy, you can execute the contents of a code block with the syntactic sugar of just the variable name followed by parenthesis (NameHash.hash("Homer")) , which is executing the call() method by default. In this case, however, you must execute the memoized function via an explicit invocation to call().

Most functional languages either include memoization or make it trivial to implement. For example, memoization is built into Clojure; you can memoize any function by using the built-in (memoize) function. For example, if you have an existing (hash) function, you can memoize it via (memoize (hash "homer")) for a caching version. Example 4-8 implements the name-hashing algorithm from Example 4-6 in Clojure.

Example 4-8. Memoization in Clojure

```
(ns name-hash.core)
(use '[clojure.string :only (join split)])


(let [alpha (into #{} (concat (map char (range (int \a) (inc (int \z))))
                              (map char (range (int \A) (inc (int \Z))))))
      rot13-map (zipmap alpha (take 52 (drop 26 (cycle alpha))))]
```

```
(defn rot13
  "Given an input string, produce the rot 13 version of
   the string. \"hello\" -> \"uryyb\""
  [s]
  (apply str (map #(get rot13-map % %) s))))

(defn name-hash [name]
  (apply str (map #(rot13 %) (split name #"\d"))))

(def name-hash-m (memoize name-hash))
```

Note that in Example 4-7, calling the memoized function requires an invocation of the call() method. In the Clojure version, the memoized method call is exactly the same on the surface, with the added indirection and caching invisible to the method's user.

Scala doesn't implement memoization directly but has a collection method named getOrElseUpdate() that handles most of the work of implementing it, as shown in Example 4-9.

Example 4-9. Memoization implementation in Scala

```
def memoize[A, B](f: A => B) = new (A => B) {
    val cache = scala.collection.mutable.Map[A, B]()
    def apply(x: A): B = cache.getOrElseUpdate(x, f(x))
  }

def nameHash = memoize(hash)
```

The getOrElseUpdate() function in Example 4-9 is the perfect operator for building a cache: it either retrieves the matching value or creates a new entry when none exists.

It is worth reiterating the importance of immutability for anything you memoize. If your memoized function relies on anything other than parameters to generate its results, you will receive unpredictable outcomes. If your memoized function has side effects, you won't be able to rely on that code executing when the cached value is returned.

 Make sure all memoized functions:

- Have no side effects
- Never rely on outside information

As runtimes become more sophisticated and we have plenty of machine resources at our disposal, advanced features such as memoization become common in just about every mainstream language. For example, although Java 8 doesn't include native memoization, it is easy to implement it atop the new lambda features.

Even if you don't care about functional languages such as Scala or Clojure, functional programming will enter your life through the langauge(s) you now use as they evolve.

Laziness

Lazy evaluation—deferral of expression evaluation for as long as possible—is a feature of many functional programming languages. Lazy collections deliver their elements as needed rather than precalculating them, offering several benefits. First, you can defer expensive calculations until they're absolutely needed. Second, you can create infinite collections, which keep delivering elements as long as they keep receiving requests. Third, lazy use of functional concepts such as map and filter enable you to generate more efficient code. Java doesn't natively support laziness until Java 8, but several frameworks and successor languages do.

Consider the snippet of pseudocode for printing the length of a list in Example 4-10.

Example 4-10. Pseudocode illustrating nonstrict evaluation

```
print length([2+1, 3*2, 1/0, 5-4])
```

If you try to execute this code, the result will vary depending on the type of programming language it's written in: *strict* or *nonstrict* (also known as lazy). In a strict programming language, executing (or perhaps even compiling) this code results in a DivByZero exception because of the list's third element. In a nonstrict language, the result is 4, which accurately reports the number of items in the list. After all, the method I'm calling is length(), not lengthAndThrowExceptionWhenDivByZero()! Haskell is one of the few nonstrict languages in common use. Alas, Java doesn't support nonstrict evaluation, but you can still take advantage of the concept of laziness in Java by deferring evaluation, and some next-generation languages are lazier than Java by default.

Lazy Iterator in Java

To build laziness, I require a data structure that supports the concept. Toward that end, consider the implementation of a *prime number* (a number divisible only by 1 and itself) in Example 4-11.

Example 4-11. Prime number finder in Java

```
package com.nealford.functionalthinking.primes;

import java.util.HashSet;
import java.util.Set;

import static java.lang.Math.sqrt;
```

```java
public class Prime {

    public static boolean isFactor(final int potential, final int number) {
        return number % potential == 0;
    }

    public static Set<Integer> getFactors(final int number) {
        Set<Integer> factors = new HashSet<>();
        factors.add(1);
        factors.add(number);
        for (int i = 2; i < sqrt(number) + 1; i++)
            if (isFactor(i, number)) {
                factors.add(i);
                factors.add(number / i);
            }
        return factors;
    }

    public static int sumFactors(final int number) {
        int sum = 0;
        for (int i : getFactors(number))
            sum += i;
        return sum;
    }

    public static boolean isPrime(final int number) {
        return sumFactors(number) == number + 1;
    }

    public static Integer nextPrimeFrom(final int lastPrime) {
        int candidate = lastPrime + 1;
        while (!isPrime(candidate)) candidate++;
        return candidate;
    }

}
```

Java's lack of native support for lazy collections doesn't mean you can't simulate one using an Iterator. For this example, using the helper in Example 4-11, I build an iterator that returns the next prime number on demand, shown in Example 4-12.

Example 4-12. Prime iterator in Java

```java
package com.nealford.ft.laziness;

import java.util.Iterator;

public class PrimeIterator implements Iterator<Integer> {
    private int lastPrime = 1;

    @Override
```

```
    public boolean hasNext() {
        return true;
    }

    @Override
    public Integer next() {
        return lastPrime = Prime.nextPrimeFrom(lastPrime);
    }

    @Override
    public void remove() {
        throw new RuntimeException("Fundamental nature of the universe exception!");
    }
}
```

Generally, developers think of iterators as using collections as backing stores, but any-thing that supports the Iterator interface qualifies. In Example 4-12, the hasNext() method always returns true because, as far as we know, the number of prime numbers is infinite. The remove() method doesn't apply here, so I throw an exception in case of accidental invocation. The workhorse method is the next() method, which handles two chores with its single line. First, it generates the next prime number based on the last one by calling the nextPrimeFrom() method that I added in Example 4-11. Second, it exploits Java's ability to assign and return in a single statement, updating the internal lastPrime field.

Totally Lazy Number Classifier

You might think that the ability to write concise, functional code isn't possible in Java until your company finally upgrades to Java 8. Although it's impossible to retrofit higher-order functions on older versions of Java, several frameworks have used generics, anonymous classes, and static imports cleverly to yield some of the benefits elucidated earlier.

Back in Chapter 2, I introduced the *number classification* problem. Totally Lazy (*https://code.google.com/p/totallylazy*) is a Java framework that bends Java syntax toward functional mechanisms, albeit in a wordy way. Consider the number classifier shown in Example 4-13.

Example 4-13. Number classifier using the Totally Lazy Java framework

```
import com.googlecode.totallylazy.Predicate;
import com.googlecode.totallylazy.Sequence;

import static com.googlecode.totallylazy.Predicates.is;
import static com.googlecode.totallylazy.numbers.Numbers.*;
import static com.googlecode.totallylazy.predicates.WherePredicate.where;

public class NumberClassifier {
    public static Predicate<Number> isFactor(Number n) {
```

```
        return where(remainder(n), is(zero));          ❶
    }

    public static Sequence<Number> getFactors(final Number n) {
        return range(1, n).filter(isFactor(n));
    }

    public static Sequence<Number> factors(final Number n) {
        return getFactors(n).memorise();
    }

    public static Number aliquotSum(Number n) {
        return subtract(factors(n).reduce(sum), n);
    }

    public static boolean isPerfect(Number n) {
        return equalTo(n, aliquotSum(n));
    }

    public static boolean isAbundant(Number n) {
        return greaterThan(aliquotSum(n), n);
    }

    public static boolean isDeficient(Number n) {
        return lessThan(aliquotSum(n), n);
    }}
```

❶   Framework supplies functions like remainder and predicates like where.

A number of static imports allow me to eliminate some prefix noise. After the static imports are completed, the code is atypical of Java yet quite readable. Totally Lazy must augment Java within the syntactic bounds of Java, which eliminates operator overloading, by adding appropriate methods. Therefore, num % i == 0 becomes where(remainder(n), is(zero))

Some of the convenient syntax found in Totally Lazy was inspired by the Hamcrest testing extension (*https://code.google.com/p/hamcrest*) for the JUnit testing framework (*http://junit.org*) and uses some of Hamcrest's classes. The isFactor() method becomes a call to the where() method, using Totally Lazy's remainder() method in conjunction with the Hamcrest is() method. Similarly, the factors() method becomes a filter() call on a range() object, and I use the now-familiar reduce() method to determine the sum. Java doesn't support operator overloading, so even subtraction becomes a method call, as shown in aliquotSum's subtract() call. Finally, the isPerfect() method uses Hamcrest's equalTo() method to determine if the aliquot sum of factors equals the number.

Totally Lazy does an excellent job of using the lowly static import in Java to facilitate quite readable code. Many developers believe that Java is a poor host for internal domain-specific languages, but Totally Lazy debunks that attitude. And it uses laziness aggressively, deferring every possible operation.

To build more traditional lazy data structures, it's useful to have higher-order functions.

Lazy Lists in Groovy

One of the common features of functional languages is the lazy list: a list whose contents are generated only as you need it. Lazy lists allow you to defer initialization of expensive resources until you absolutely need them. They also allow the creation of infinite sequences: lists that have no upper bound. If you aren't required to say up front how big the list could be, you can let it be as big as it needs to be.

First, I illustrate using a lazy list in Groovy in Example 4-14, and then I'll show you the implementation.

Example 4-14. Using lazy lists in Groovy

```
def prepend(val, closure) { new LazyList(val, closure) }

def integers(n) { prepend(n, { integers(n + 1) }) }

@Test
public void lazy_list_acts_like_a_list() {
    def naturalNumbers = integers(1)
    assertEquals('1 2 3 4 5 6 7 8 9 10', naturalNumbers.getHead(10).join(' '))
    def evenNumbers = naturalNumbers.filter { it % 2 == 0 }
    assertEquals('2 4 6 8 10 12 14 16 18 20', evenNumbers.getHead(10).join(' '))
}
```

The first method in Example 4-14, prepend(), creates a new LazyList, allowing you to prepend values. Readers familiar with functional languages might know this method as cons(), used to *construct* lists. The next method, integers(), returns a list of integers by using the prepend() method. The two parameters I send to the prepend() method are the initial value of the list and a code block that includes code to generate the next value. The integers() method acts like a factory that returns the lazy list of integers with a value at the front and a way to calculate additional values in the rear.

To retrieve values from the list, I call the getHead() method, which returns the argument number of values from the top of the list. In Example 4-14, naturalNumbers is a lazy sequence of all integers. To get a subset of them, I call the getHead() method, specifying how many integers I want. As the assertion indicates, I receive a list of the first 10 natural numbers. Using the filter() method, I retrieve a lazy list of even numbers and call the getHead() method to fetch the first 10 even numbers.

The implementation of LazyList appears in Example 4-15.

Example 4-15. LazyList implementation

```
package com.nealford.ft.allaboutlists

class LazyList {
    private head, tail

    LazyList(head, tail) {
        this.head = head;
        this.tail = tail
    }

    def LazyList getTail() { tail ? tail() : null }

    def List getHead(n) {
        def harvestedValues = [];
        def current = this
        n.times {
            harvestedValues << current.head
            current = current.tail
        }
        harvestedValues
    }

    def LazyList filter(Closure p) {
        if (p(head))
            p.owner.prepend(head, { getTail().filter(p) })
        else
            getTail().filter(p)
    }
}
```

A lazy list holds a head and tail, specified in the constructor. The getTail() method ensures that tail isn't null and executes it. The getHead() method gathers the elements that I want to return, one at a time, pulling the existing element off the head of the list and asking the tail to generate a new value. The call to n.times {…} performs this operation for the number of elements requested, and the method returns the harvested values.

Lazy lists work great in situations in which generating resources are expensive, such as generating a list of perfect numbers.

Lazy list of perfect numbers

I discuss my favorite guinea-pig examples, *perfect numbers*, in Chapter 2. One of the shortcomings of all the implementations so far is the need to specify the number for classification. Instead, I want a version that returns a lazy list of perfect numbers. Toward that goal, I've written a highly functional, very compact perfect-number finder that supports lazy lists, shown in Example 4-16.

Example 4-16. Pared-down version of perfect-number classifier in Groovy

```groovy
package com.nealford.ft.allaboutlists

import static com.nealford.ft.allaboutlists.NumberClassification.*

def enum NumberClassification {
  PERFECT, ABUNDANT, DEFICIENT
}

class NumberClassifier {
  static def factorsOf(number) {
    (1..number).findAll { i -> number % i == 0 }
  }

  static def classify(number) {
    switch (factorsOf(number).inject(0, { i, j -> i + j })) {
      case { it < 2 * number }: return DEFICIENT
      case { it > 2 * number }: return ABUNDANT
      case { it == 2 * number }: return PERFECT
    }
  }

  static def isPerfect(number) {
    classify(number) == PERFECT
  }


  static def nextPerfectNumberAfter(n) {
    while (!isPerfect(++n));
    n
  }
}
```

In Example 4-16, I create a compact `classify()` method, using the `NumberClassifi cation` enumeration as the return value and checking each of the number classification rules against the implicit value `it`. I make use of the one new method, `nextPerfect Number()`, which in turn uses the `isPerfect()` method to find the next perfect number beyond the number passed as the parameter. This method call will take a long time to execute even for small values (especially given how unoptimized this code is); there just aren't that many perfect numbers.

Using this new version of `NumberClassifier`, I can create a lazy list of perfect numbers, as shown in Example 4-17.

Example 4-17. Lazily initialized list of perfect numbers

```groovy
def perfectNumbers(n) { prepend(n,
  { perfectNumbers(nextPerfectNumberAfter(n)) }) };

@Test
```

```
public void infinite_perfect_number_sequence() {
    def perfectNumbers = perfectNumbers(nextPerfectNumberAfter(1))
    assertEquals([6, 28, 496], perfectNumbers.getHead(3))
}
```

Using the `prepend()` method I defined in Example 4-15, I construct a list of perfect numbers with the initial value as the head and a closure block that knows how to calculate the next perfect number as the tail. I initialize my list with the first perfect number after 1 (using a static import so that I can call my `NumberClassifier.nextPerfectNum herFrom()` method more easily), then I ask my list to return the first three perfect numbers.

Calculating new perfect numbers is expensive, so I would rather do it as little as possible. By building it as a lazy list, I can defer calculations until the optimum time.

It is more difficult to think about infinite sequences if your abstraction of "list" is "numbered slots." Thinking of a list as the "first element" and the "rest of the list" encourages you to think of the elements in the list rather than the structure, which in turn allows you to think about things like lazy lists.

Building a Lazy List

As already mentioned, languages can be categorized as *strict* (eagerly evaluating all expressions) or *lazy* (deferring evaluation until absolutely needed). Groovy is a strict language by nature, but I can transform a nonlazy list into a lazy one by recursively wrapping a strict list within a closure. This lets me defer evaluation of subsequent values by delaying execution of the closure block.

A strict empty list in Groovy is represented by an array, using empty square braces: [ ]. If I wrap it in a closure, it becomes a lazy empty list:

```
{-> [] }
```

If I need to add an a element to the list, I can add it to the front, then make the entire new list lazy again:

```
{-> [ a, {-> [] } ] }
```

The method for adding to the front of the list is traditionally called either `prepend` or `cons`. To add more elements, I repeat this operation for each new item; adding three elements (a, b, and c) to the list yields:

```
{-> [a, {-> [b, {-> [ c, {-> [] } ] } ] } ] }
```

This syntax is clumsy, but once I understand the principle, I can create a class in Groovy that implements a traditional set of methods for a lazy collection, as shown in Example 4-18.

Example 4-18. Building a lazy list in Groovy

```groovy
class PLazyList {
  private Closure list

  private PLazyList(list) {
    this.list = list
  }

  static PLazyList nil() {
    new PLazyList({-> []})
  }

  PLazyList cons(head) {
    new PLazyList({-> [head, list]})
  }

  def head() {
    def lst = list.call()
    lst ? lst[0] : null
  }

  def tail() {
    def lst = list.call()
    lst ? new PLazyList(lst.tail()[0]) : nil()
  }

  boolean isEmpty() {
    list.call() == []
  }

  def fold(n, acc, f) {
    n == 0 || isEmpty() ? acc : tail().fold(n - 1, f.call(acc, head()), f)
  }

  def foldAll(acc, f) {
    isEmpty() ? acc : tail().foldAll(f.call(acc, head()), f)
  }

  def take(n) {
    fold(n, []) {acc, item -> acc << item}
  }

  def takeAll() {
    foldAll([]) {acc, item -> acc << item}
  }

  def toList() {
    takeAll()
  }
}
```

In Example 4-18, the constructor is private; it's called by starting with an empty list using `nil()`, which constructs an empty list. The `cons()` method enables me to add new elements by prepending the passed parameter, then wrapping the result in a closure block.

The next three methods enable list traversal. The `head()` method returns the first element of the list, and `tail()` returns the sublist of all elements except the first. In both cases, I `call()` the closure block—known as forcing the evaluation in lazy terms. Because I'm retrieving values, it ceases to be lazy as I harvest the values. Not surprisingly, the `isEmpty()` method checks to see if any terms are left to resolve.

The remaining methods are higher-order functions for performing operations on the list. The `fold()` and `foldAll()` methods perform the familiar *fold* operation. I've shown the use of this family of methods in previous chapters, but this is the first time I've shown a recursive definition written purely in terms of closure blocks. The `foldAll()` method checks to see if the list is empty and, if it is, returns `acc` (the accumulator, the seed value for the fold operation). Otherwise, it recursively calls `foldAll()` on the `tail()` of the list, passing the accumulator and the head of the list. The function (the `f` parameter) should accept two parameters and yield a single result; this is the "fold" operation as you fold one element atop the adjacent one.

Example 4-19 shows how to build and manipulate a list.

Example 4-19. Exercising lazy lists

```
def lazylist = PLazyList.nil().cons(4).cons(3).cons(2).cons(1)
println(lazylist.takeAll())
println(lazylist.foldAll(0, {i, j -> i + j}))
lazylist = PLazyList.nil().cons(1).cons(2).cons(4).cons(8)
println(lazylist.take(2))
```

In Example 4-19, I create a list by `cons()`-ing values onto an empty list. Notice that when I `takeAll()` of the elements, they come back in the reverse order of their addition to the list. Remember, `cons()` is really shorthand for *prepend*; it adds elements to the front of the list. The `foldAll()` method enables me to sum the list by providing a transformation code block, `{i, j -> i + j}`, which uses addition as the fold operation. Last, I use the `take()` method to force evaluation of only the first two elements.

Real-world lazy-list implementations differ from this one, avoiding recursion and adding more flexible manipulation methods. However, knowing conceptually what's happening inside the implementation aids understanding and use.

Benefits of Laziness

Lazy lists have several benefits. First, you can use them to create infinite sequences. Because the values aren't evaluated until needed, you can model infinite lists by using lazy collections, as I illustrated in Example 4-16.

A second benefit is reduced storage size. If—rather than hold an entire collection—I can derive subsequent values, then I can trade storage for execution speed. Choosing to use a lazy collection becomes a trade-off between the expense of storing the values versus calculating new ones.

Third, one of the key benefits of lazy collections is that the runtime can generate more efficient code. Consider the code in Example 4-20.

Example 4-20. Finding palindromes in Groovy

```
def isPalindrome(s) {
  def sl = s.toLowerCase()
  sl == sl.reverse()
}

def findFirstPalindrome(s) {
  s.tokenize(' ').find {isPalindrome(it)}
}

s1 = "The quick brown fox jumped over anna the dog";
println(findFirstPalindrome(s1))
s2 = "Bob went to Harrah and gambled with Otto and Steve"
println(findFirstPalindrome(s2))
```

The isPalindrome() method in Example 4-20 normalizes the case of the subject word, then determines if the word has the same characters in reverse. findFirstPalin drome() tries to find the first palindrome in the passed string by using Groovy's find() method, which accepts a code block as the filtering mechanism.

Suppose I have a huge sequence of characters within which I need to find the first palindrome. During the execution of the findFirstPalindrome() method, the code in Example 4-20 first eagerly tokenizes the entire sequence, creating an intermediate data structure, then issues the find() command. Groovy's tokenize() method isn't lazy, so in this case it might build a huge temporary data structure, only to discard most of it. Consider the same code written in Clojure, appearing in Example 4-21.

Example 4-21. Clojure's palindromes

```
(defn palindrome? [s]
  (let [sl (.toLowerCase s)]
  (= sl (apply str (reverse sl)))))

(defn find-palindromes [s]
  (filter palindrome? (clojure.string/split s #" ")))
```

```
(println (find-palindromes "The quick brown fox jumped over anna the dog"))
; (anna)
(println (find-palindromes "Bob went to Harrah and gambled with Otto and Steve"))
;(Bob Harrah Otto)
(println (take 1 (find-palindromes "Bob went to Harrah with Otto and Steve")))
;(Bob)
```

The implementation details in Examples 4-20 and 4-21 are the same but use different language constructs. In the Clojure (`palindrome?`) function, I make the parameter string lowercase, then check equality with the reversed string. The extra call to `apply` converts the character sequence returned by reverse back to a `String` for comparison. The (`find-palindromes`) function uses Clojure's (`filter`) function, which accepts a function to act as the filter and the collection to be filtered. For the call to the (`palindrome?`) function, Clojure provides several alternatives. I can create an anonymous function to call it as (`palindrome? %`). When I have a single parameter, Clojure allows me to avoid declaring the anonymous function and naming the parameter, which I substitute with % in the (`palindrome? %`) function call. In Example 4-21, I can use the even shorter form of the function name directly; (`filter`) is expecting a method that accepts a single parameter and returns a Boolean, which matches (`palindrome?`).

The translation from Groovy to Clojure entailed more than just syntax. All of Clojure's data structures are lazy when possible, including operations on collections such as `filter` and `split`. Thus, in the Clojure version, everything is automatically lazy, which manifests in the second example in Example 4-21, when I call (`find-palindromes`) on the collection with multiples. The return from (`filter`) is a lazy collection that is forced as I print it. If I want only the first entry, I must take the number of lazy entrants that I need from the list.

Scala approaches laziness in a slightly different way. Rather than make everything lazy by default, it offers lazy views on collections. Consider the Scala implementation of the palindrome problem in Example 4-22.

Example 4-22. Scala palindromes

```
def isPalindrome(x: String) = x == x.reverse
def findPalidrome(s: Seq[String]) = s find isPalindrome

findPalindrome(words take 1000000)
```

In Example 4-22, pulling one million words from the collection via the `take` method will be quite inefficient, especially if the goal is to find the first palindrome. To convert the `words` collection to a lazy one, use the `view` method:

```
findPalindrome(words.view take 1000000)
```

The view method allows lazy traversal of the collection, making for more efficient code.

Lazy Field Initialization

Before leaving the subject of laziness, I'll mention that two languages have a nice facility to make expensive initializations lazy. By prepending lazy onto the val declaration, you can convert fields in Scala from eager to as-needed evaluation:

```
lazy val x = timeConsumingAndOrSizableComputation()
```

This is basically syntactic sugar for the code:

```
var _x = None
def x = if (_x.isDefined) _x.get else {
  _x = Some(timeConsumingAndOrSizableComputation())
  _x.get
}
```

Groovy has a similar facility using an advanced language feature known as *Abstract Syntax Tree* (AST) transformations. They enable you to interact with the compiler's generation of the underlying abstract syntax tree, allowing user transformations at a low level. One of the predefined transformations is the @Lazy attribute, shown in action in Example 4-23.

Example 4-23. Lazy fields in Groovy

```
class Person {
    @Lazy pets = ['Cat', 'Dog', 'Bird']
}

def p = new Person()
assert !(p.dump().contains('Cat'))

assert p.pets.size() == 3
assert p.dump().contains('Cat')
```

In Example 4-23, the Person instance p doesn't appear to have a Cat value until the data structure is accessed the first time. Groovy also allows you to use a closure block to initialize the data structure:

```
class Person {
    @Lazy List pets = { /* complex computation here */ }()
}
```

Finally, you can also tell Groovy to use soft references—Java's version of a pointer reference that can be reclaimed if needed—to hold your lazily initialized field:

```
class Person {
    @Lazy(soft = true) List pets = ['Cat', 'Dog', 'Bird']
}
```

This creates the most memory efficient version, with lazy initialization and aggressive reclamation of memory if needed.

CHAPTER 5

Evolve

Functional programming languages approach code reuse differently from object-oriented languages. Object-oriented languages tend to have many data structures with many operations, whereas functional languages exhibit few data structures with many operations. Object-oriented languages encourage you to create class-specific methods, and you can capture recurring patterns for later reuse. Functional languages help you achieve reuse by encouraging the application of common transformations to data structures, with higher-order functions to customize the operation for specific instances.

In this chapter, I cover various ways that languages have *evolved* solutions to particular recurring problems in software. I discuss the attitudinal change in functional programming with respect to custom data structures; talk about the malleability of languages and solutions; and cover dispatch options, operator overloading, and functional data structures.

Few Data Structures, Many Operations

> It is better to have 100 functions operate on one data structure than 10 functions on 10 data structures.
>
> — Alan Perlis

In object-oriented imperative programming languages, the units of reuse are classes and the messages they communicate with, typically captured in a class diagram. The seminal work in that space, *Design Patterns: Elements of Reusable Object-Oriented Software* (Addison-Wesley, 1994), includes at least one class diagram with each pattern. In the OOP world, developers are encouraged to create unique data structures, with specific operations attached in the form of methods. Functional programming languages don't try to achieve reuse in the same way. They prefer a few key data structures (such as list, set, and map) with highly optimized operations on those data structures. You pass data structures plus higher-order functions to "plug into" this machinery, customizing it for a particular use. For example, the `filter()` function I've shown in several languages accepts a code block as the "plug-in" higher-order function that determines the filter criteria, and the machinery applies the filter criteria in an efficient way, returning the filtered list.

Encapsulation at the function level enables reuse at a more granular, fundamental level than building custom class structures. One advantage of this approach is already appearing in Clojure. For example, consider the case of parsing XML. A huge number of frameworks exist for this task in Java, each with custom data structures and method semantics (for example, SAX versus DOM). Clojure parses XML into a standard `Map` structure, rather than encouraging you to use a custom data structure. Because Clojure includes lots of tools for working with maps, performing XPath-style queries is simple using the built-in list-comprehension function, `for`, as shown in Example 5-1.

Example 5-1. Parsing XML in Clojure

```
(use 'clojure.xml)

(def WEATHER-URI "http://weather.yahooapis.com/forecastrss?w=%d&u=f")

(defn get-location [city-code]
  (for [x (xml-seq (parse (format WEATHER-URI city-code)))
        :when (= :yweather:location (:tag x))]
    (str (:city (:attrs x)) "," (:region (:attrs x)))))

(defn get-temp [city-code]
  (for [x (xml-seq (parse (format WEATHER-URI city-code)))
        :when (= :yweather:condition (:tag x))]
    (:temp (:attrs x))))

(println "weather for " (get-location 12770744) "is " (get-temp 12770744))
```

In Example 5-1, I access Yahoo!'s weather service to fetch a given city's weather forecast. Because Clojure is a Lisp variant, it's easiest to read inside out. The actual call to the service endpoint occurs at `(parse (format WEATHER-URI city-code))`, which uses `String`'s `format()` function to embed the `city-code` into the string. The list comprehension function, `for`, places the parsed XML, cast using `xml-seq` into a queryable map named x. The `:when` predicate determines the match criteria; in this case, I'm searching for a tag (translated into a Clojure keyword) `:yweather:condition`.

To understand the syntax used to pull values from the data structure, it's useful to see what's in it. When parsed, the pertinent call to the weather service returns the data structure shown in this excerpt:

```
({:tag :yweather:condition, :attrs {:text Fair, :code 34, :temp 62, :date Tue,
  04 Dec 2012 9:51 am EST}, :content nil})
```

Because Clojure is optimized to work with maps, keywords become functions on the maps that contain them. The call in Example 5-1 to (:tag x) is shorthand for "retrieve the value corresponding to the :tag key from the map stored in x." Thus, :yweather:condition yields the maps values associated with that key, which includes the attrs map that I fetch the :temp value from using the same syntax.

One of the initially daunting details in Clojure is the seemingly endless ways to interact with maps and other core data structures. However, it's a reflection of the fact that most things in Clojure try to resolve to these core, optimized data structures. Rather than trap parsed XML in a unique framework, it tries instead to convert it to an existing structure that already has tools in place.

An advantage of the reliance on fundamental data structures appears in the XML libraries in Clojure. For traversing tree-shaped structures (such as XML documents), a useful data structure called a *zipper* was created in 1997. A zipper allows you to navigate trees structurally by providing coordinate directions. For example, starting from the root of the tree, you can issue commands such as (→ z/down z/down z/left) to navigate to the second-level left element. Functions already exist in Clojure to convert parsed XML into a zipper, enabling consistent navigation across all tree-shaped structures.

Bending the Language Toward the Problem

Most developers labor under the misconception that their job is to take a complex business problem and translate it into a language such as Java. They do that because Java isn't particularly flexible as a language, forcing you to mold your ideas into the rigid structure already there. But as developers use malleable languages, they see the opportunity to bend the language more toward their problem rather than the problem toward their language. Languages like Ruby—with its friendlier-than-mainstream support for domain-specific languages (DSLs)—demonstrated that potential. Modern functional languages go even further. Scala was designed to accommodate hosting internal DSLs, and all Lisps (including Clojure) have unparalleled flexibility in enabling the developer to mold the language to the problem. For instance, Example 5-2 uses the XML primitives in Scala to implement Example 5-1's weather example.

Example 5-2. Scala's syntactic sugar for XML

```
import scala.xml._
import java.net._
import scala.io.Source

val theUrl = "http://weather.yahooapis.com/forecastrss?w=12770744&u=f"

val xmlString = Source.fromURL(new URL(theUrl)).mkString
val xml = XML.loadString(xmlString)
```

```
val city = xml \\ "location" \\ "@city"
val state = xml \\ "location" \\ "@region"
val temperature = xml \\ "condition" \\ "@temp"

println(city + ", " + state + " " + temperature)
```

Scala was designed for malleability, allowing extensions such as operator overloading (covered on page 91) and implicit types. In Example 5-2, Scala is extended to allow XPath-like queries using the \\ operator.

While not specifically a functional language feature, the ability to gracefully mold your language closer to your problem domain is common in modern languages and facilitates a functional, declarative style of coding.

 Evolve your program toward the problem, not the other way around.

Rethinking Dispatch

Chapter 3 introduced the concept of Scala *pattern matching*, one example of an alternative dispatch mechanism, which I'm using as a broad term to describe ways languages dynamically choose behavior. This section extends the discussion to show how dispatch mechanisms in various functional JVM languages enable more conciseness and flexibility than their Java counterparts.

Improving Dispatch with Groovy

In Java, conditional execution ends up using the `if` statement except in very limited cases where the `switch` statement applies. Because long series of `if` statements become difficult to read, Java developers often rely on the Gang of Four (GoF) *Factory* (or *Abstract Factory*) pattern. If you use a language that includes a more flexible decision expression, you can simplify a lot of your code without resorting to the extra structure of patterns.

Groovy has a powerful `switch` statement that mimics the syntax—but not the behavior—of Java's `switch` statement, as shown in Example 5-3.

Example 5-3. Groovy's vastly improved switch statement

```
package com.nealford.ft.polydispatch

class LetterGrade {
  def gradeFromScore(score) {
    switch (score) {
```

```
      case 90..100 : return "A"
      case 80..<90 : return "B"
      case 70..<80 : return "C"
      case 60..<70 : return "D"
      case 0..<60  : return "F"
      case ~"[ABCDFabcdf]" : return score.toUpperCase()
      default: throw new IllegalArgumentException("Invalid score: ${score}")
    }
  }
}
```

The code in Example 5-3 accepts a `score` and returns the corresponding letter grade. Unlike Java, Groovy's `switch` statement accepts a wide variety of dynamic types. In Example 5-3, the `score` parameter should be either a number between 0 and 100 or a letter grade. As in Java, you must terminate each case with either a `return` or `break`, following the same fall-through semantics. But in Groovy, unlike Java, I can specify ranges (`90..100`, noninclusive ranges (`80..<90`), regular expressions (`~"[ABCD Fabcdf]"`), and a default condition.

Groovy's dynamic typing enables me to send different types of parameters and react appropriately, as shown in the unit tests in Example 5-4.

Example 5-4. Testing Groovy letter grades

```
import org.junit.Test
import com.nealford.ft.polydispatch.LetterGrade

import static org.junit.Assert.assertEquals

class LetterGradeTest {
  @Test
  public void test_letter_grades() {
    def lg = new LetterGrade()
    assertEquals("A", lg.gradeFromScore(92))
    assertEquals("B", lg.gradeFromScore(85))
    assertEquals("D", lg.gradeFromScore(65))
    assertEquals("F", lg.gradeFromScore("f"))
  }
}
```

A more powerful `switch` gives you a useful middle ground between serial `if`s and the Factory design pattern. Groovy's `switch` lets you match ranges and other complex types, which is similar in intent to pattern matching in Scala.

Clojure's "Bendable" Language

Java and languages like it include *keywords*—the syntactic scaffolding of the language. Developers can't create new keywords in the language (although some Java-like languages allow extension via metaprogramming), and keywords have semantics unavailable to developers. For example, the Java if statement "understands" things like short-circuit Boolean evaluation. Although you can create functions and classes in Java, you can't create fundamental building blocks, so you need to translate problems into the syntax of the programming language. (In fact, many developers think their job is to perform this translation.) In Lisp variants such as Clojure, the developer can modify the language toward the problem, blurring the distinction between what the language designer and developers using the language can create.

In Clojure, developers use the language to create readable (Lisp) code. For instance, Example 5-5 shows the letter-grade example in Clojure.

Example 5-5. Letter grades in Clojure

```
(ns lettergrades)

(defn in [score low high]
  (and (number? score) (<= low score high))))

(defn letter-grade [score]
  (cond
    (in score 90 100) "A"
    (in score 80 90)  "B"
    (in score 70 80)  "C"
    (in score 60 70)  "D"
    (in score 0 60)   "F"
    (re-find #"[ABCDFabcdf]" score) (.toUpperCase score)))
```

In Example 5-5, I wrote the letter-grade function to read nicely, then implemented the in function to make it work. In this code, the cond function enables me to evaluate a sequence of tests, handled by my in function. As in the previous examples, I handle both numeric and existing letter-grade strings. Ultimately, the return value should be an uppercase character, so if the input is in lowercase, I call the toUpperCase function on the returned string. In Clojure, functions are first-class citizens rather than classes, making function invocations "inside-out": the call to score.toUpperCase() in Java is equivalent to Clojure's (.toUpperCase score).

I test Clojure's letter-grade implementation in Example 5-6.

Example 5-6. Testing Clojure letter grades

```
(ns nealford-test
  (:use clojure.test)
  (:use lettergrades))

(deftest numeric-letter-grades
  (dorun (map #(is (= "A" (letter-grade %))) (range 90 100)))
  (dorun (map #(is (= "B" (letter-grade %))) (range 80 89)))
  (dorun (map #(is (= "C" (letter-grade %))) (range 70 79)))
  (dorun (map #(is (= "D" (letter-grade %))) (range 60 69)))
  (dorun (map #(is (= "F" (letter-grade %))) (range 0 59))))
```

```
(deftest string-letter-grades
  (dorun (map #(is (= (.toUpperCase %)
              (letter-grade %))) ["A" "B" "C" "D" "F" "a" "b" "c" "d" "f"])))
```

```
(run-all-tests)
```

In this case, the test code is more complex than the implementation! However, it shows how concise Clojure code can be.

In the numeric-letter-grades test, I want to check every value in the appropriate ranges. Reading inside out, the code #(is (= "A" (letter-grade %))) creates a new anonymous function that takes a single parameter and returns true if the correct letter grade returns. The map function maps this anonymous function across the collection in the second parameter, which is the list of numbers within the appropriate range.

The (dorun) function allows side effects to occur, which the testing framework relies on. Calling map across each range in Example 5-6 returns a list of all true values. The (is) function from the clojure.test namespace verifies the value as a side effect. Calling the mapping function within (dorun) allows the side effect to occur correctly and execute the tests.

Clojure Multimethods and a la carte Polymorphism

A long series of if statements is hard to read and debug, yet Java doesn't have any particularly good alternatives at the language level. This problem is typically solved by using either the Factory or Abstract Factory design patterns from the GoF. The Factory Pattern works in Java because of class-based polymorphism, allowing me to define a general method signature in a parent class or interface, then choose the implementation that executes dynamically.

Many developers dismiss Clojure because it isn't an object-oriented language, believing that object-oriented languages are the pinnacle of power. That's a mistake: Clojure has all the features of an object-oriented language, implemented independently of other features. For example, Clojure supports polymorphism but isn't restricted to evaluating the class to determine dispatch. Clojure supports polymorphic multimethods whereby dispatch is triggered by whatever characteristic (or combination) the developer wants.

In Clojure, data typically resides in structs, which mimic the data part of classes. Consider the Clojure code in Example 5-7.

Example 5-7. Defining a color structure in Clojure

```
(defstruct color :red :green :blue)
```

```
(defn red [v]
  (struct color v 0 0))
```

```
(defn green [v]
  (struct color 0 v 0))

(defn blue [v]
  (struct color 0 0 v))
```

In Example 5-7, I define a structure that holds three values, corresponding to color values. I also create three methods that return a structure saturated with a single color.

A *multimethod* in Clojure is a method definition that accepts a dispatch function, which returns the decision criteria. Subsequent definitions allow you to flesh out different versions of the method. Example 5-8 shows a multimethod definition.

Example 5-8. Defining a multimethod

```
(defn basic-colors-in [color]
  (for [[k v] color :when (not= v 0)] k))

(defmulti color-string basic-colors-in)

(defmethod color-string [:red] [color]
  (str "Red: " (:red color)))

(defmethod color-string [:green] [color]
  (str "Green: " (:green color)))

(defmethod color-string [:blue] [color]
  (str "Blue: " (:blue color)))

(defmethod color-string :default [color]
  (str "Red:" (:red color) ", Green: " (:green color) ", Blue: " (:blue color)))
```

In Example 5-8, I define a dispatch function called `basic-colors-in`, which returns a vector of all nonzero color values. For the variations on the method, I specify what should happen if the dispatch function returns a single color; in this case, it returns a string with its color. The last case includes the optional `:default` keyword, which handles remaining cases. For this one, I cannot assume that I received a single color, so the return lists the values of all the colors.

Tests to exercise these multimethods appear in Example 5-9.

Example 5-9. Testing colors in Clojure

```
(ns color-dispatch.core-test
  (:require [clojure.test :refer :all]
            [color-dispatch.core :refer :all]))

(deftest pure-colors
  (is (= "Red: 5" (color-string (struct color 5 0 0))))
  (is (= "Green: 12" (color-string (struct color 0 12 0))))
  (is (= "Blue: 40" (color-string (struct color 0 0 40)))))
```

```
(deftest varied-colors
  (is (= "Red:5, Green: 40, Blue: 6" (color-string (struct color 5 40 6))))))

(run-all-tests)
```

In Example 5-9, when I call the method with a single color, it executes the singular color version of the multimethod. If I call it with a complex color profile, the default method returns all colors.

Decoupling polymorphism from inheritance provides a powerful, contextualized dispatch mechanism. For example, consider the problem of image file formats, each one having a different set of characteristics to define the type. By using a dispatch function, Clojure enables you to build powerful dispatch as contextualized as Java polymorphism but with fewer limitations.

Operator Overloading

A common feature of functional languages is operator overloading—the ability to redefine operators (such as +, -, or *) to work with new types and exhibit new behaviors. Omission of operator overloading was a conscious decision during Java's formative period, but virtually every modern language now features it, including the natural successors to Java.

Groovy

Groovy tries to update Java's syntax while preserving its natural semantics. Thus, Groovy allows operator overloading by automatically mapping operators to method names. For example, if you want to overload the + operator on the `Integer` class, you override its `plus()` method. The entire list of mappings is available online; Table 5-1 shows a partial list.

Table 5-1. Partial list of Groovy operator/method mappings

Operator	Method
x + y	x.plus(y)
x * y	x.multiply(y)
x / y	x.div(y)
x ** y	x.power(y)

As an example of operator overloading, I'll create a `ComplexNumber` class in both Groovy and Scala. Complex numbers are a mathematical concept with both a real and imaginary part, typically written as, for example, 3 + 4i. Complex numbers are common in many scientific fields, including engineering, physics, electromagnetism, and chaos theory.

Developers writing applications in those fields greatly benefit from the ability to create operators that mirror their problem domain.

A Groovy `ComplexNumber` class appears in Example 5-10.

Example 5-10. ComplexNumber in Groovy

```
package complexnums

class ComplexNumber {
   def real, imaginary

   public ComplexNumber(real, imaginary) {
     this.real = real
     this.imaginary = imaginary
   }

   def plus(rhs) {
     new ComplexNumber(this.real + rhs.real, this.imaginary + rhs.imaginary)
   }
   // formula: (x + yi)(u + vi) = (xu - yv) + (xv + yu)i.
   def multiply(rhs) {
     new ComplexNumber(
         real * rhs.real - imaginary * rhs.imaginary,
         real * rhs.imaginary + imaginary * rhs.real)
   }

   def String toString() {
     real.toString() + ((imaginary < 0 ? "" : "+") + imaginary + "i").toString()
   }
}
```

In Example 5-10, I create a class that holds both real and imaginary parts, and I create the overloaded `plus()` and `multiply()` operators. Adding two complex numbers is straightforward: the `plus()` operator adds the two numbers' respective real and imaginary parts to each other to produce the result. Multiplying two complex numbers requires this formula:

$$(x + yi)(u + vi) = (xu - yv) + (xv + yu)i$$

The `multiply()` operator in Example 5-10 replicates the formula. It multiplies the numbers' real parts, then subtracts the product of the imaginary parts, which is added to the product of the real and imaginary parts both multiplied by each other.

Example 5-11 exercises the new complex-number operators.

Example 5-11. Testing complex-number operators

```
package complexnums

import org.junit.Test
import static org.junit.Assert.assertTrue
```

```
import org.junit.Before

class ComplexNumberTest {
  def x, y

  @Before void setup() {
    x = new ComplexNumber(3, 2)
    y = new ComplexNumber(1, 4)
  }

  @Test void plus() {
    def z = x + y;
    assertTrue 3 + 1 == z.real
    assertTrue 2 + 4 == z.imaginary
  }

  @Test void multiply() {
    def z = x * y
    assertTrue(-5  == z.real)
    assertTrue 14 == z.imaginary
  }

  @Test void to_string() {
    assertTrue "3+2i" == x.toString()
    assertTrue "4+6i" == (x + y).toString()
    assertTrue "3+0i" == new ComplexNumber(3, 0).toString()
    assertTrue "4-2i" == new ComplexNumber(4, -2).toString()
  }
}
```

In Example 5-11, the plus() and multiply() test methods' use of the overloaded operators—both of which are represented by the same symbols that the domain experts use—is indistinguishable from similar use of built-in types.

Scala

Scala allows operator overloading by discarding the distinction between operators and methods: operators are merely methods with special names. Thus, to override the multiplication operator in Scala, you override the * method. I create complex numbers in Scala in Example 5-12.

Example 5-12. Complex numbers in Scala

```
final class Complex(val real: Int, val imaginary: Int) extends Ordered[Complex] {

  def +(operand: Complex) =
      new Complex(real + operand.real, imaginary + operand.imaginary)

  def +(operand: Int) =
    new Complex(real + operand, imaginary)
```

```
  def -(operand: Complex) =
    new Complex(real - operand.real, imaginary - operand.imaginary)

  def -(operand: Int) =
    new Complex(real - operand, imaginary)

  def *(operand: Complex) =
      new Complex(real * operand.real - imaginary * operand.imaginary,
          real * operand.imaginary + imaginary * operand.real)

  override def toString() =
      real + (if (imaginary < 0) "" else "+") + imaginary + "i"

  override def equals(that: Any) = that match {
    case other : Complex => (real == other.real) && (imaginary == other.imaginary)
    case other : Int => (real == other) && (imaginary == 0)
    case _ => false
  }

  override def hashCode(): Int =
    41 * ((41 + real) + imaginary)

  def compare(that: Complex) : Int = {
    def myMagnitude = Math.sqrt(real ^ 2 + imaginary ^ 2)
    def thatMagnitude = Math.sqrt(that.real ^ 2 + that.imaginary ^ 2)
    (myMagnitude - thatMagnitude).round.toInt
  }
}
```

The class in Example 5-12 includes real and imaginary members, as well as the plus and multiply operators/functions. In Scala, constructor parameters appear as class parameters; my class accepts `real` and `imaginary` parts. Because Scala automatically provides fields, the remainder of the class contains method definitions. For plus, minus, and multiply, I declare eponymous methods that accept `Complex` numbers as parameters.

The `toString()` method in Example 5-12 exemplifies another bit of common ground among many functional languages: use of expressions rather than statements. In the `toString()` method, I must supply the + sign if the imaginary part is positive, but the real part's sign will suffice otherwise. In Scala, `if` is an expression rather than a statement, eliminating the need for Java's ternary operator (`?:`).

I can use `ComplexNumbers` naturally, as shown in Example 5-13.

Example 5-13. Using complex numbers in Scala

```
import org.scalatest.FunSuite

class ComplexTest extends FunSuite {

  def fixture =
    new {
```

```
    val a = new Complex(1, 2)
    val b = new Complex(30, 40)
  }

  test("plus") {
    val f = fixture
    val z = f.a + f.b
    assert(1 + 30 == z.real)
  }

  test("comparison") {
    val f = fixture
    assert(f.a < f.b)
    assert(new Complex(1, 2) >= new Complex(3, 4))
    assert(new Complex(1, 1) < new Complex(2,2))
    assert(new Complex(-10, -10) > new Complex(1, 1))
    assert(new Complex(1, 2) >= new Complex(1, 2))
    assert(new Complex(1, 2) <= new Complex(1, 2))
  }

}
```

Java's designers explicitly decided against operator overloading, feeling from their experience with C++ that it added too much complexity. Most modern languages have removed much of the definitional complexity, but the warning against abuse still resonates.

 Overload operators to *bend* your language toward an existing problem domain, not to create a brand new language.

Functional Data Structures

In Java, errors are traditionally handled by exceptions and the language's support for creating and propagating them. But what if structured exception handling didn't exist? Many functional languages don't support the exception paradigm, so they must find alternate ways of expressing error conditions.

Exceptions violate a couple of premises that most functional languages adhere to. First, they prefer *pure* functions, which have no side effects. However, throwing an exception is a side effect that causes unusual (exceptional) program flow. Functional languages tend to deal with *values*, preferring to react to return values that indicate an error rather than interrupt program flow.

The other feature that functional programs tend toward is *referential transparency*: the calling routine shouldn't care whether it accesses a value or a function that returns a value. If a function can also throw an exception, it isn't a safe substitute for a value.

In this section, I show type-safe, error-handling mechanisms in Java that bypass the normal exception-propagation mechanism (with assistance in some examples from the Functional Java framework).

Functional Error Handling

If you want to handle errors in Java without using exceptions, the fundamental obstacle is the language limitation of a single return value from methods. But methods can, of course, return a single `Object` (or subclass) reference, which can hold multiple values. So I could enable multiple return values by using a `Map`. Consider the `divide()` method in Example 5-14.

Example 5-14. Using Map to handle multiple returns

```java
public static Map<String, Object> divide(int x, int y) {
    Map<String, Object> result = new HashMap<String, Object>();
    if (y == 0)
        result.put("exception", new Exception("div by zero"));
    else
        result.put("answer", (double) x / y);
    return result;
}
```

In Example 5-14, I create a `Map` with `String` as the key and `Object` as the value. In the `divide()` method, I put either `exception` to indicate failure or `answer` to indicate success. Both modes are tested in Example 5-15.

Example 5-15. Testing success and failure with Maps

```java
@Test
public void maps_success() {
    Map<String, Object> result = RomanNumeralParser.divide(4, 2);
    assertEquals(2.0, (Double) result.get("answer"), 0.1);
}

@Test
public void maps_failure() {
    Map<String, Object> result = RomanNumeralParser.divide(4, 0);
    assertEquals("div by zero", ((Exception) result.get("exception")).getMessage());
}
```

In Example 5-15, the `maps_success` test verifies that the correct entry exists in the returned `Map`. The `maps_failure` test checks for the exception case.

This approach has some obvious problems. First, whatever ends up in the Map isn't type-safe, which disables the compiler's ability to catch certain errors. Enumerations for the keys would improve this situation slightly, but not much. Second, the method invoker doesn't know if the method call was a success, placing the burden on the caller to check the dictionary of possible results. Third, nothing prevents both keys from having values, which makes the result ambiguous.

What I need is a mechanism that allows me to return two (or more) values in a type-safe way.

The Either Class

The need to return two distinct values occurs frequently in functional languages, and a common data structure used to model this behavior is the Either class. Either is designed to hold either a left or right value (but never both). This data structure is referred to as a *disjoint union*. Some C-based languages contain the *union* data type, which can hold one instance of several different types. A disjoint union has slots for two types but holds an instance for only one of them.

Scala includes an instance of Either, as shown in Example 5-16.

Example 5-16. Scala's predefined Either class

```
type Error = String
type Success = String
def call(url:String):Either[Error,Success]={
    val response = WS.url(url).get.value.get
    if (valid(response))
        Right(response.body)
    else Left("Invalid response")
}
```

As Example 5-16 shows, a common use for Either is for error handling. Either integrates nicely into the overall Scala ecosystem; a popular case includes pattern matching on an instance of Either, as shown in Example 5-17.

Example 5-17. Scala Either and pattern matching

```
getContent(new URL("http://nealford.com")) match {
  case Left(msg) => println(msg)
  case Right(source) => source.getLines.foreach(println)
}
```

Even though it isn't built into the Java language, I can create a substitute using generics; I create a simple Either class, as shown in Example 5-18.

Example 5-18. Returning two (type-safe) values via the Either class

```
package com.nealford.ft.errorhandling;

public class Either<A,B> {
    private A left = null;
    private B right = null;

    private Either(A a,B b) {
        left = a;
        right = b;
    }

    public static <A,B> Either<A,B> left(A a) {
        return new Either<A,B>(a,null);
    }

    public A left() {
        return left;
    }

    public boolean isLeft() {
        return left != null;
    }

    public boolean isRight() {
        return right != null;
    }

    public B right() {
        return right;
    }

    public static <A,B> Either<A,B> right(B b) {
        return new Either<A,B>(null,b);
    }

    public void fold(F<A> leftOption, F<B> rightOption) {
        if(right == null)
            leftOption.f(left);
        else
            rightOption.f(right);
    }
}
```

In Example 5-18, the Either class has a private constructor, making construction the responsibility of either of the two static methods left(A a) or right(B b). The remaining methods in the class are helpers that retrieve and investigate the class members.

Armed with Either, I can write code that returns either an exception or a legitimate result (but never both) while retaining type safety. The common functional convention is that the *left* of an `Either` class contains an exception (if any), and the *right* contains the result.

Parsing Roman numerals

To illustrate the use of `Either`, I have a class named `RomanNumeral` that appears in Example 5-19.

Example 5-19. Naive implementation of Roman numerals in Java

```
package com.nealford.ft.errorhandling;

public class RomanNumeral {

    private static final String NUMERAL_MUST_BE_POSITIVE =
            "Value of RomanNumeral must be positive.";
    private static final String NUMERAL_MUST_BE_3999_OR_LESS =
            "Value of RomanNumeral must be 3999 or less.";
    private static final String DOES_NOT_DEFINE_A_ROMAN_NUMERAL =
            "An empty string does not define a Roman numeral.";
    private static final String NO_NEGATIVE_ROMAN_NUMERALS =
            "Negative numbers not allowed";
    private static final String NUMBER_FORMAT_EXCEPTION =
            "Illegal character in Roman numeral.";

    private final int num;

    private static int[] numbers = {1000, 900, 500, 400, 100, 90,
            50, 40, 10, 9, 5, 4, 1};
    private static String[] letters = {"M", "CM", "D", "CD", "C", "XC",
            "L", "XL", "X", "IX", "V", "IV", "I"};


    public RomanNumeral(int arabic) {
        if (arabic < 1)
            throw new NumberFormatException(NUMERAL_MUST_BE_POSITIVE);
        if (arabic > 3999)
            throw new NumberFormatException(NUMERAL_MUST_BE_3999_OR_LESS);
        num = arabic;
    }


    public RomanNumeral(String roman) {
        if (roman.length() == 0)
            throw new NumberFormatException(DOES_NOT_DEFINE_A_ROMAN_NUMERAL);
        if (roman.charAt(0) == '-')
            throw new NumberFormatException(NO_NEGATIVE_ROMAN_NUMERALS);

        roman = roman.toUpperCase();

        int positionInString = 0;
        int arabicEquivalent = 0;
```

```
    while (positionInString < roman.length()) {
        char letter = roman.charAt(positionInString);
        int number = letterToNumber(letter);
        if (number < 0)
            throw new NumberFormatException(NUMBER_FORMAT_EXCEPTION);
        positionInString++;
        if (positionInString == roman.length())
            arabicEquivalent += number;
        else {
            int nextNumber = letterToNumber(roman.charAt(positionInString));
            if (nextNumber > number) {
                arabicEquivalent += (nextNumber - number);
                positionInString++;
            } else
                arabicEquivalent += number;
        }
    }

    if (arabicEquivalent > 3999)
        throw new NumberFormatException(NUMERAL_MUST_BE_3999_OR_LESS);
    num = arabicEquivalent;
}

private int letterToNumber(char letter) {
    switch (letter) {
        case 'I':
            return 1;
        case 'V':
            return 5;
        case 'X':
            return 10;
        case 'L':
            return 50;
        case 'C':
            return 100;
        case 'D':
            return 500;
        case 'M':
            return 1000;
        default:
            return -1;
    }
}

public String toString() {
    String romanNumeral = "";
    int remainingPartToConvert = num;
    for (int i = 0; i < numbers.length; i++) {
        while (remainingPartToConvert >= numbers[i]) {
            romanNumeral += letters[i];
            remainingPartToConvert -= numbers[i];
```

```
            }
        }
        return romanNumeral;
    }

    public int toInt() {
        return num;
    }
}
```

I also have a class named `RomanNumeralParser` that calls the `RomanNumeral` class. The `parseNumber()` method and illustrative tests appear in Example 5-20.

Example 5-20. Parsing Roman numerals

```
public static Either<Exception, Integer> parseNumber(String s) {
    if (! s.matches("[IVXLXCDM]+"))
        return Either.left(new Exception("Invalid Roman numeral"));
    else
        return Either.right(new RomanNumeral(s).toInt());
}
```

I can verify the results via tests, as shown in Example 5-21.

Example 5-21. Testing parse of Roman numerals

```
@Test
public void parsing_success() {
    Either<Exception, Integer> result = RomanNumeralParser.parseNumber("XLII");
    assertEquals(Integer.valueOf(42), result.right());
}

@Test
public void parsing_failure() {
    Either<Exception, Integer> result = RomanNumeralParser.parseNumber("FOO");
    assertEquals(INVALID_ROMAN_NUMERAL, result.left().getMessage());
}
```

In Example 5-21, the `parseNumber()` method performs an astoundingly naive validation (for the purpose of showing an error), placing the error condition in the `Either`'s left or the result in its right. Both cases are shown in the unit tests.

This is a big improvement over passing `Map` data structures around. I retain type safety (note that I can make the exception as specific as I like); the errors are obvious in the method declaration via the generics; and my results come back with one extra level of indirection, unpacking the result (whether exception or answer) from `Either`. And the extra level of indirection enables laziness.

Lazy parsing and Functional Java

The Either class appears in many functional algorithms and is so common in the functional world that the Functional Java framework contains an implementation of Either that would work in Examples 5-18 and 5-20. But it was made to work with other Functional Java constructs. Accordingly, I can use a combination of Either and Functional Java's P1 class to create lazy error evaluation.

In Functional Java, a P1 class is a simple wrapper around a single method named _1() that takes no parameters. (Other variants—P2, P3, etc.—hold multiple methods.) A P1 is used in Functional Java to pass a code block around without executing it, enabling you to execute the code in a context of your choosing, substituting for a higher-order function.

In Java, exceptions are instantiated as soon as you throw an exception. By returning a lazily evaluated method, I can defer the creation of the exception until a later time. Consider the example and associated tests in Example 5-22.

Example 5-22. Using Functional Java to create a lazy parser

```java
public static P1<Either<Exception, Integer>> parseNumberLazy(final String s) {
    if (! s.matches("[IVXLXCDM]+"))
        return new P1<Either<Exception, Integer>>() {
            public Either<Exception, Integer> _1() {
                return Either.left(new Exception("Invalid Roman numeral"));
            }
        };
    else
        return new P1<Either<Exception, Integer>>() {
            public Either<Exception, Integer> _1() {
                return Either.right(new RomanNumeral(s).toInt());
            }
        };
}
```

The test appears in Example 5-23.

Example 5-23. Testing Functional Java–based lazy parser

```java
@Test
public void parse_lazy() {
    P1<Either<Exception, Integer>> result =
            RomanNumeralParser.parseNumberLazy("XLII");
    assertEquals(42, result._1().right().intValue());
}

@Test
public void parse_lazy_exception() {
    P1<Either<Exception, Integer>> result =
            RomanNumeralParser.parseNumberLazy("FOO");
    assertTrue(result._1().isLeft());
```

```
    assertEquals(INVALID_ROMAN_NUMERAL, result._1().left().getMessage());
}
```

The code in Example 5-22 is similar to Example 5-20, with an extra P1 wrapper. In the parse_lazy test, I must unpack the result via the call to _1() on the result, which returns Either's *right*, from which I can retrieve the value. In the parse_lazy_exception test, I can check for the presence of a *left*, and I can unpack the exception to discern its message.

The exception (along with its expensive-to-generate stack trace) isn't created until you unpack Either's left with the _1() call. Thus, the exception is lazy, letting you defer execution of the exception's constructor.

Providing defaults

Laziness isn't the only benefit of using Either for error handling. Another is that you can provide default values. Consider the code in Example 5-24.

Example 5-24. Providing reasonable default return values

```
private static final int MIN = 0;
private static final int MAX = 1000;

    public static Either<Exception, Integer> parseNumberDefaults(final String s) {
    if (! s.matches("[IVXLXCDM]+"))
        return Either.left(new Exception("Invalid Roman numeral"));
    else {
        int number = new RomanNumeral(s).toInt();
        return Either.right(new RomanNumeral(number >= MAX ? MAX : number).toInt());
    }
}
```

The corresponding tests that illustrate default values appear in Example 5-25.

Example 5-25. Testing defaults

```
@Test
public void parse_defaults_normal() {
    Either<Exception, Integer> result =
        RomanNumeralParser.parseNumberDefaults("XLII");
    assertEquals(42, result.right().intValue());
}
@Test
public void parse_defaults_triggered() {
    Either<Exception, Integer> result =
        RomanNumeralParser.parseNumberDefaults("MM");
    assertEquals(1000, result.right().intValue());
}
```

In Example 5-25, let's assume that I never allow any Roman numerals greater than MAX, and any attempt to set one greater will default to MAX. parseNumberDefaults() ensures that the default is placed in Either's *right*.

Wrapping exceptions

I can also use Either to wrap exceptions, converting structured exception handling to functional, as shown in Example 5-26.

Example 5-26. Catching other people's exceptions

```
public static Either<Exception, Integer> divide(int x, int y) {
    try {
        return Either.right(x / y);
    } catch (Exception e) {
        return Either.left(e);
    }
}
```

Tests that illustrate wrapping exceptions appear in Example 5-27.

Example 5-27. Testing wrapping exceptions

```
@Test
public void catching_other_people_exceptions() {
    Either<Exception, Integer> result = FjRomanNumeralParser.divide(4, 2);
    assertEquals((long) 2, (long) result.right().value());
    Either<Exception, Integer> failure = FjRomanNumeralParser.divide(4, 0);
    assertEquals("/ by zero", failure.left().value().getMessage());
}
```

In Example 5-26, I attempt division, potentially raising an ArithmeticException. If an exception occurs, I wrap it in Either's *left*; otherwise I return the result in *right*. Using Either enables you to convert traditional exceptions (including checked ones) into a more functional style.

Of course, you can also lazily wrap exceptions thrown from called methods, as shown in Example 5-28.

Example 5-28. Lazily catching exceptions

```
public static P1<Either<Exception, Integer>> divideLazily(final int x, final int y) {
    return new P1<Either<Exception, Integer>>() {
        public Either<Exception, Integer> _1() {
            try {
                return Either.right(x / y);
            } catch (Exception e) {
                return Either.left(e);
            }
        }
    }
```

```
    };
}
```

Example 5-29 shows tests around lazily catching exceptions.

Example 5-29. Example of handling thrown exceptions

```
@Test
public void lazily_catching_other_peoples_exceptions() {
    P1<Either<Exception, Integer>> result = FjRomanNumeralParser.divideLazily(4, 2);
    assertEquals((long) 2, (long) result._1().right().value());
    P1<Either<Exception, Integer>> failure = FjRomanNumeralParser.divideLazily(4, 0);
    assertEquals("/ by zero", failure._1().left().value().getMessage());
}
```

Modeling `Either` in Java is cumbersome because it doesn't natively include the concept, so I must resort to generics and classes to model it by hand. Languages like Scala have `Either` and similar constructs built in. Languages like Clojure and Groovy don't include something like `Either` natively because it's easy to generate values in a dynamically typed language. For example, in Clojure, rather than create a specific two-part data structure, you'd likely return a *keyword*, a Clojure constant string used to symbolically identify things.

The Option Class

`Either` is a handy generic two-part return concept, useful for building generic structures (such as tree-shaped data structures, shown later in this chapter). For the specific case of returning results from a function, a similar class to `Either` exists in several languages and frameworks called `Option`, which provides a simpler exception case: either none, indicating no legitimate value, or some, indicating successful return. `Option` from Functional Java (*http://functionaljava.org*) is demonstrated in Example 5-30.

Example 5-30. Using Option

```
public static Option<Double> divide(double x, double y) {
    if (y == 0)
        return Option.none();
    return Option.some(x / y);
}
```

Example 5-31 shows an `Option` class appearing in tests.

Example 5-31. Testing Option behavior

```
@Test
public void option_test_success() {
    Option result = FjRomanNumeralParser.divide(4.0, 2);
    assertEquals(2.0, (Double) result.some(), 0.1);
}
```

```
@Test
public void option_test_failure() {
    Option result = FjRomanNumeralParser.divide(4.0, 0);
    assertEquals(Option.none(), result);
}
```

As illustrated in Example 5-30, an Option contains either none() or some(), similar to left and right in Either but specific to methods that might not have a legitimate return value. The Option class is considered a simpler subset of Either; Option typically holds success or failure, whereas Either can hold anything.

Either Trees and Pattern Matching

In this section, I continue my exploration of Either, using it to build tree-shaped structures—which in turn enables me to mimic Scala's pattern matching for building traversal methods.

Using generics in Java, an Either becomes a single data structure that accepts either of two types, which it stores in left and right parts.

In the previous section's Roman numeral parser example, Either holds either an Ex ception (*left*) or an Integer (*right*), as illustrated in Figure 5-1.

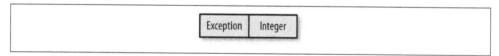

Figure 5-1. The Either abstraction holding either of two types

In that example, this assignment populates the Either:

```
Either<Exception, Integer> result = RomanNumeralParser.parseNumber("XLII");
```

I will use this data structure to create a tree-shaped structure, but first I need to cover *pattern matching* to illustrate the benefit of a data structure like Either.

Scala pattern matching

One of the nice features of Scala is the ability to use pattern matching for dispatch. It's easier to show than to describe, so consider the function in Example 5-32 , which converts numerical scores to letter grades.

Example 5-32. Using Scala pattern matching to assign letter grades based on score

```
val VALID_GRADES = Set("A", "B", "C", "D", "F")

def letterGrade(value: Any) : String = value match {
  case x:Int if (90 to 100).contains(x) => "A"
  case x:Int if (80 to 90).contains(x) => "B"
```

```
    case x:Int if (70 to 80).contains(x) => "C"
    case x:Int if (60 to 70).contains(x) => "D"
    case x:Int if (0 to 60).contains(x) => "F"
    case x:String if VALID_GRADES(x.toUpperCase) => x.toUpperCase
}
```

Statements that illustrate letter grade evaluation at work appear in Example 5-33.

Example 5-33. Testing letter grades

```
printf("Amy scores %d and receives %s\n", 91, letterGrade(91))
printf("Bob scores %d and receives %s\n", 72, letterGrade(72))
printf("Sam never attened class, scored %d, and received %s\n",
    44, letterGrade(44))
printf("Roy transfered and already had %s, which translated as %s\n",
    "B", letterGrade("B"))
```

In Example 5-32, the entire body of the function consists of match applied to a value. For each of the options, a pattern guard enables me to filter the matches based on criteria in addition to the argument's type. The advantage of this syntax is a clean partitioning of the options instead of a cumbersome series of if statements.

Pattern matching works in conjunction with Scala's *case classes*, which are classes with specialized properties—including the ability to perform pattern matching—to eliminate decision sequences. Consider matching color combinations, as shown in Example 5-34.

Example 5-34. Matching case classes in Scala

```
class Color(val red:Int, val green:Int, val blue:Int)

case class Red(r:Int) extends Color(r, 0, 0)
case class Green(g:Int) extends Color(0, g, 0)
case class Blue(b:Int) extends Color(0, 0, b)

def printColor(c:Color) = c match {
  case Red(v) => println("Red: " + v)
  case Green(v) => println("Green: " + v)
  case Blue(v) => println("Blue: " + v)
  case col:Color => {
    print("R: " + col.red + ", ")
    print("G: " + col.green + ", ")
    println("B: " + col.blue)
  }

  case null => println("invalid color")
}
```

In Example 5-34, I create a base Color class, then create specialized single color versions as case classes. When determining which color was passed to the function, I use match to pattern match against all the possible options, including the last case, which handles null.

Java doesn't have pattern matching, so it can't replicate Scala's ability to create cleanly readable dispatch code. But marrying generics and well-known data structures brings it close, which brings me back to `Either`.

Either trees

It is possible to model a tree data structure with three abstractions, as shown in Table 5-2.

Table 5-2. Building a tree with three abstractions

Tree abstraction	Description
empty	Cell has no value
leaf	Cell has a value of a particular data type
node	Points to other *leafs* or *nodes*

For convenience, I use the `Either` class from the Functional Java framework. Conceptually, the `Either` abstraction expands into as many slots as needed. For example, consider the declaration `Either<Empty, Either<Leaf, Node>>`, which creates a three-part data structure like the one shown in Figure 5-2.

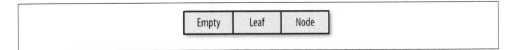

Figure 5-2. Either<Empty, Either<Leaf, Node>> data structure

Armed with an `Either` implementation of the three tree abstractions, I define a tree as shown in Example 5-35.

Example 5-35. Tree based on Either

```
package com.nealford.ft.structuralpatternmatching;

import fj.data.Either;
import static fj.data.Either.left;
import static fj.data.Either.right;

public abstract class Tree {
    private Tree() {}

    public abstract Either<Empty, Either<Leaf, Node>> toEither();

    public static final class Empty extends Tree {
        public Either<Empty, Either<Leaf, Node>> toEither() {
            return left(this);
        }

        public Empty() {}
    }

    public static final class Leaf extends Tree {
        public final int n;

        @Override
        public Either<Empty, Either<Leaf, Node>> toEither() {
            return right(Either.<Leaf, Node>left(this));
        }

        public Leaf(int n) { this.n = n; }
    }

    public static final class Node extends Tree {
        public final Tree left;
        public final Tree right;
```

```
        public Either<Empty, Either<Leaf, Node>> toEither() {
            return right(Either.<Leaf, Node>right(this));
        }

        public Node(Tree left, Tree right) {
            this.left = left;
            this.right = right;
        }
    }

}
```

The abstract Tree class in Example 5-35 defines within it three final concrete classes:
Empty, Leaf, and Node. Internally, the Tree class uses the three-slotted Either shown
in Figure 5-2, enforcing the convention that the leftmost slot always holds Empty, the
middle slot holds a Leaf, and the rightmost slot holds a Node. It does this by requiring
each class to implement the toEither() method, returning the appropriate "slot" for
that type. Each "cell" in the data structure is a union in the traditional computer science
sense, designed to hold only one of the three possible types at any given time.

Given this tree structure and the fact that I know that its internal structure is based on
<Either, <Left, Node>>, I can mimic pattern matching for visiting each element in
the tree.

Pattern matching for tree traversal

Scala's pattern matching encourages you to think about discrete cases. The left() and
right() methods of Functional Java's Either implementation both implement the
Iterable interface; this enables me to write pattern-matching-inspired code, as shown
in Example 5-36, to determine the tree's depth.

Example 5-36. Checking a tree's depth using pattern-matching-like syntax

```
static public int depth(Tree t) {
    for (Empty e : t.toEither().left())
        return 0;
    for (Either<Leaf, Node> ln: t.toEither().right()) {
        for (Leaf leaf : ln.left())
            return 1;
        for (Node node : ln.right())
            return 1 + max(depth(node.left), depth(node.right));
    }
    throw new RuntimeException("Inexhaustible pattern match on tree");
}
```

The depth() method in Example 5-36 is a recursive depth-finding function. Because
my tree is based on a specific data structure (<Either, <Left, Node>>), I can treat each
"slot" as a specific case. If the cell is empty, this branch has no depth. If the cell is a

leaf, I count it as a tree level. If the cell is a node, I know that I should recursively search both left and right sides, adding a 1 for another level of recursion.

I can also use the same pattern-matching syntax to perform a recursive search of the tree, as shown in Example 5-37.

Example 5-37. Determining presence in a tree

```
static public boolean inTree(Tree t, int value) {
    for (Empty e : t.toEither().left())
        return false;
    for (Either<Leaf, Node> ln: t.toEither().right()) {
        for (Leaf leaf : ln.left())
            return value == leaf.n;
        for (Node node : ln.right())
            return inTree(node.left, value) | inTree(node.right, value);
    }
    return false;
}
```

As before, I specify the return value for each possible "slot" in the data structure. If I encounter an empty cell, I return `false`; my search has failed. For a `leaf`, I check the passed value, returning `true` if they match. Otherwise, when encountering a `node`, I recurse through the tree, using the | (non-short-circuited or operator) to combine the returned Boolean values.

To see tree creation and searching in action, consider the unit test in Example 5-38.

Example 5-38. Testing tree searchability

```
@Test
public void more_elaborate_searchp_test() {
    Tree t = new Node(new Node(new Node(new Node(
            new Node(new Leaf(4),new Empty()),
            new Leaf(12)), new Leaf(55)),
            new Empty()), new Leaf(4));
    assertTrue(inTree(t, 55));
    assertTrue(inTree(t, 4));
    assertTrue(inTree(t, 12));
    assertFalse(inTree(t, 42));
}
```

In Example 5-38, I build a tree, then investigate whether elements are present. The `inTree()` method returns `true` if one of the leaves equals the search value, and the `true` propagates up the recursive call stack because of the | operator, as shown in Example 5-37.

The code in Example 5-37 determines if an element appears in the tree. A more sophisticated version also checks for the number of occurrences, as shown in Example 5-39.

Example 5-39. Finding number of occurrences in a tree

```
static public int occurrencesIn(Tree t, int value) {
    for (Empty e: t.toEither().left())
        return 0;
    for (Either<Leaf, Node> ln: t.toEither().right()) {
        for (Leaf leaf : ln.left())
            if (value == leaf.n) return 1;
        for (Node node : ln.right())
            return occurrencesIn(node.left, value)
                    + occurrencesIn(node.right, value);
    }
    return 0;
}
```

In Example 5-39, I return 1 for every matching leaf, allowing me to count the number of occurrences of each number in the tree.

The code in Example 5-40 illustrates tests for depth(), inTree(), and occurrence sIn() for a complex tree.

Example 5-40. Testing depth, presence, and occurrences in complex trees

```
@Test
public void multi_branch_tree_test() {
    Tree t = new Node(new Node(new Node(new Leaf(4),
            new Node(new Leaf(1), new Node(
                    new Node(new Node(new Node(
            new Node(new Node(new Leaf(10), new Leaf(0)),
                    new Leaf(22)), new Node(new Node(
                            new Node(new Leaf(4), new Empty()),
                            new Leaf(101)), new Leaf(555))),
                            new Leaf(201)), new Leaf(1000)),
                    new Leaf(4)))),
            new Leaf(12)), new Leaf(27));
    assertEquals(12, depth(t));
    assertTrue(inTree(t, 555));
    assertEquals(3, occurrencesIn(t, 4));
}
```

Because I've imposed regularity on the tree's internal structure, I can analyze the tree during traversal by thinking individually about each case, reflected in the type of element. Although not as expressive as full-blown Scala pattern matching, the syntax comes surprisingly close to the Scala ideal.

CHAPTER 6

Advance

If the primary paradigm that your language supports is objects, it's easy to start thinking about solutions to every problem in those terms. However, most modern languages are multiparadigm, meaning that they support object, metaobject, functional, and other paradigms. Learning to use different paradigms for suitable problems is part of the evolution toward being a better developer.

Design Patterns in Functional Languages

Some contingents in the functional world claim that the concept of the design pattern is flawed and isn't needed in functional programming. A case can be made for that view under a narrow definition of pattern—but that's an argument more about semantics than use. The concept of a design pattern—a named, cataloged solution to a common problem—is alive and well. However, patterns sometimes take different guises under different paradigms. Because the building blocks and approaches to problems are different in the functional world, some of the traditional Gang of Four patterns disappear, while others preserve the problem but solve it radically differently.

In the functional programming world, traditional design patterns generally manifest in one of three ways:

- The pattern is absorbed by the language.
- The pattern solution still exists in the functional paradigm, but the implementation details differ.
- The solution is implemented using capabilities other languages or paradigms lack. (For example, many solutions that use metaprogramming are clean and elegant—and they're not possible in Java.)

I'll investigate these three cases in turn.

Function-Level Reuse

Composition—in the form of passed parameters plus first-class functions—appears frequently in functional programming libraries as a reuse mechanism. Functional languages achieve reuse at a coarser-grained level than object-oriented languages, extracting common machinery with parameterized behavior. Object-oriented systems consist of objects that communicate by sending messages to (or, more specifically, executing methods on) other objects. Figure 6-1 represents an object-oriented system.

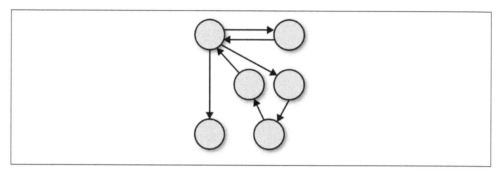

Figure 6-1. Reuse in an object-oriented system

When you discover a useful collection of classes and their corresponding messages, you extract that graph of classes for reuse, as shown in Figure 6-2.

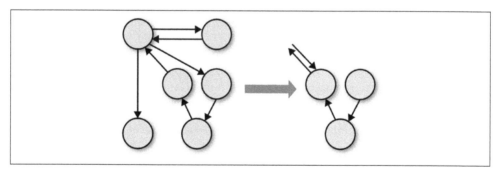

Figure 6-2. Extracting useful parts of the graph

Not surprisingly, one of most popular books in the software-engineering world is *Design Patterns: Elements of Reusable Object-Oriented Software* (Addison-Wesley, 1994), a catalog of exactly the type of extraction shown in Figure 6-2. Reuse via patterns is so pervasive that numerous other books also catalog (and provide distinct names for) such extractions. The design-patterns movement has been a tremendous boon to the software development world because it supplies nomenclature and exemplars. But, fundamentally, reuse via design patterns is fine-grained: one solution (the Flyweight Pattern, for example) is orthogonal to another (the Memento Pattern). Each of the problems solved by design patterns is highly specific, which makes patterns useful because you can often find a pattern that matches your current problem—but narrowly useful because it is so specific to the problem.

Functional programmers also want reusable code, but they use different building blocks. Rather than try to create well-known relationships (coupling) between structures, functional programming tries to extract coarse-grained reuse mechanisms—based in part on category theory, a branch of mathematics that defines relationships (morphism) between types of objects. Most applications do things with lists of elements, so a functional approach is to build reuse mechanisms around the idea of lists plus contextualized, portable code. Functional languages rely on first-class functions (functions that can appear anywhere any other language construct can appear) as parameters and return values. Figure 6-3 illustrates this concept.

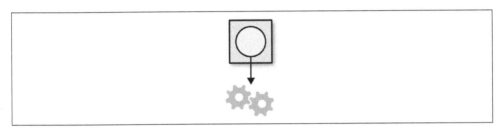

Figure 6-3. Reuse via coarse-grained mechanisms plus portable code

In Figure 6-3, the gear box represents abstractions that deal generically with some fundamental data structure, and the yellow box represents portable code, encapsulating data inside it.

The functional approach to filtering lists illustrated in Example 2-12 is common across functional programming languages and libraries. Using the ability to pass code as a parameter (as to the `filter()` method) illustrates thinking about code reuse in a different way. If you come from a traditional design-patterns–driven object-oriented world, you are likely more accustomed to building classes and methods to solve problems.

However, functional languages allow you to cede some scaffolding and boilerplate with the same conceptual result. For example, the Command design pattern isn't needed in a language with closures. Ultimately, that design pattern only exists to address language deficiencies, such as the inability to pass behavior without wrapping it in a (generally) useless skeleton class. Of course, the Command design pattern also supports other useful behavior, such as *undo*, but it is predominantly used as a way to pass executable chunks of code to methods.

Another common pattern that loses most of its boilerplate code is the Template Method design pattern, introduced in Chapter 3.

Template Method

First-class functions make the Template Method design pattern simpler to implement, because they remove potentially unnecessary structure. Template Method defines the skeleton of an algorithm in a method, deferring some steps to subclasses and forcing them to define those steps without changing the algorithm's structure. A typical implementation of the Template Method appears in Example 6-1, in Groovy.

Example 6-1. "Standard" Template Method implementation

```
package templates;

abstract class Customer {
    def plan

    def Customer() {
        plan = []
    }

    def abstract checkCredit()
    def abstract checkInventory()
    def abstract ship()

    def process() {
        checkCredit()
        checkInventory()
        ship()
    }
}
```

In Example 6-1, the `process()` method relies on `checkCredit()`, `checkInventory()`, and `ship()`, whose definitions must be supplied by subclasses because they are abstract methods.

Because first-class functions can act as any other data structure, I can redefine the code in Example 6-1 using code blocks, as shown in Example 6-2.

Example 6-2. Template Method with first-class functions

```
package templates;

class CustomerBlocks {
    def plan, checkCredit, checkInventory, ship

    def CustomerBlocks() {
        plan = []
    }
```

```
    def process() {
        checkCredit()
        checkInventory()
        ship()
    }
}
```

In Example 6-2, the steps in the algorithm are merely properties of the class, assignable like any other property. This is an example in which the language feature mostly absorbs the implementation details. It's still useful to talk about this pattern as a solution (deferring steps to subsequent handlers) to a problem, but the implementation is simpler.

The two solutions aren't equivalent. In the "traditional" Template Method shown in Example 6-1, the abstract class requires subclasses to implement the dependent methods. Of course, the subclass might just create an empty method body, but the abstract-method definition forms a kind of documentation, reminding subclassers to take it into account. On the other hand, the rigidity of method declarations might not be suitable in situations in which more flexibility is required. For example, I could create a version of my Customer class that accepts any list of methods for processing.

Deep support for features such as code blocks makes languages developer-friendly. Consider the case in which you want to allow subclassers to skip some of the steps. Groovy has a special protected access operator (?.) that ensures that the object isn't null before invoking a method on it. Consider the process() definition in Example 6-3.

Example 6-3. Adding protection to code-block invocation

```
def process() {
  checkCredit?.call()
  checkInventory?.call()
  ship?.call()
}
```

In Example 6-3, whoever implements the functions assigned to the checkCredit, check Inventory, and ship properties can choose which of them to leave blank. Syntactic sugar like the ?. operator allows developers to cede repetitive, obfuscating code such as a long series of if blocks to the language, replacing boilerplate code with expressiveness. Although there is nothing particularly functional about the ?. operator, it serves as a good example of ceding busywork to the runtime.

The availability of higher-order functions allows you to avoid unnecessary boilerplate code in the most common uses of classic design patterns such as Command and Template.

Strategy

A popular design pattern simplified by first-class functions is the Strategy pattern. Strategy defines a family of algorithms, encapsulating each one and making them interchangeable. It lets the algorithm vary independently from clients that use it. First-class functions make it simple to build and manipulate strategies.

A traditional implementation of the Strategy design pattern, for calculating the products of numbers, appears in Example 6-4.

Example 6-4. Using the Strategy design pattern for products of two numbers

```
interface Calc {
  def product(n, m)
}

class CalcMult implements Calc {
  def product(n, m) { n * m }
}

class CalcAdds implements Calc {
  def product(n, m) {
    def result = 0
    n.times {
      result += m
    }
    result
  }
}
```

In Example 6-4, I define an interface for the product of two numbers. I implement the interface with two different concrete classes (strategies): one using multiplication and the other using addition. To test these strategies, I create a test case, shown in Example 6-5.

Example 6-5. Testing product strategies

```
class StrategyTest {
  def listOfStrategies = [new CalcMult(), new CalcAdds()]

  @Test
  public void product_verifier() {
    listOfStrategies.each { s ->
      assertEquals(10, s.product(5, 2))
    }
  }
}
```

As expected in Example 6-5, both strategies return the same value. Using code blocks as first-class functions, I can reduce much of the ceremony from the previous example. Consider the case of exponentiation strategies, shown in Example 6-6.

Example 6-6. Testing exponentiation with less ceremony

```
@Test
public void exp_verifier() {
  def listOfExp = [
      {i, j -> Math.pow(i, j)},
      {i, j ->
        def result = i
        (j-1).times { result *= i }
        result
      }]

  listOfExp.each { e ->
    assertEquals(32, e(2, 5))
    assertEquals(100, e(10, 2))
    assertEquals(1000, e(10, 3))
  }
}
```

In Example 6-6, I define two strategies for exponentiation directly inline, using Groovy code blocks, trading formality for convenience. The traditional approach forces name and structure around each strategy, which is sometimes desirable. However, note that I have the option to add more stringent safeguards to the code in Example 6-6, whereas I can't easily bypass the restrictions imposed by the more traditional approach—which is more of a dynamic-versus-static argument than a functional-programming-versus-design-patterns one.

The Flyweight Design Pattern and Memoization

The Flyweight pattern is an optimization technique that uses sharing to support a large number of fine-grained object references. You keep a pool of objects available, creating references into the pool for particular views.

Flyweight uses the idea of a canonical object—a single representative object that represents all other objects of that type. For example, if you have a particular consumer product, a canonical version of the product represents all products of that type.

In an application, instead of creating a list of products for each user, you create one list of canonical products, and each user has a reference into that list for his product.

Consider the classes in Example 6-7, which model computer types.

Example 6-7. Simple classes modeling types of computers

```
class Computer {
  def type
  def cpu
  def memory
  def hardDrive
  def cd
```

```
  }

class Desktop extends Computer {
  def driveBays
  def fanWattage
  def videoCard
}

class Laptop extends Computer {
  def usbPorts
  def dockingBay
}

class AssignedComputer {
  def computerType
  def userId

  public AssignedComputer(computerType, userId) {
    this.computerType = computerType
    this.userId = userId
  }
}
```

In these classes, let's say it's inefficient to create a new `Computer` instance for each user, assuming that all the computers have the same specifications. An `AssignedComputer` associates a computer with a user.

A common way to make this code more efficient combines the Factory and Flyweight patterns. Consider the singleton factory for generating canonical computer types, shown in Example 6-8.

Example 6-8. Singleton factory for flyweight computer instances

```
class CompFactory {
  def types = [:]
  static def instance;

  private ComputerFactory() {
    def laptop = new Laptop()
    def tower = new Desktop()
    types.put("MacBookPro6_2", laptop)
    types.put("SunTower",  tower)
  }

  static def getInstance() {
    if (instance == null)
      instance = new CompFactory()
    instance
  }

  def ofType(computer) {
    types[computer]
```

```
  }
}
```

The `ComputerFactory` class builds a cache of possible computer types, then delivers the proper instance via its `ofType()` method. This is a traditional singleton factory as you would write it in Java.

However, Singleton is a design pattern as well, and it serves as another good example of a pattern ceded to the runtime. Consider the simplified `ComputerFactory`, which uses the `@Singleton` annotation provided by Groovy, shown in Example 6-9.

Example 6-9. Simplified singleton factory

```
@Singleton class ComputerFactory {
  def types = [:]

  private ComputerFactory() {
    def laptop = new Laptop()
    def tower = new Desktop()
    types.put("MacBookPro6_2", laptop)
    types.put("SunTower",  tower)
  }

  def ofType(computer) {
    types[computer]
  }
}
```

To test that the factory returns canonical instances, I write a unit test, shown in Example 6-10.

Example 6-10. Testing canonical types

```
@Test
public void comp_factory() {
  def bob = new AssignedComputer(
    CompFactory.instance.ofType("MacBookPro6_2"), "Bob")
  def steve = new AssignedComputer(
    CompFactory.instance.ofType("MacBookPro6_2"), "Steve")
  assertTrue(bob.computerType == steve.computerType)
}
```

Saving common information across instances is a good idea, and it's an idea that I want to preserve as I cross into functional programming. However, the implementation details are quite different. This is an example of preserving the semantics of a pattern while changing (preferably, simplifying) the implementation.

As I covered in Chapter 4, a memoized function allows the runtime to cache the values for you. Consider the functions defined in Example 6-11.

Example 6-11. Memoization of flyweights

```
def computerOf = {type ->
  def of = [MacBookPro6_2: new Laptop(), SunTower: new Desktop()]
  return of[type]
}

def computerOfType = computerOf.memoize()
```

In Example 6-11, the canonical types are defined within the `computerOf` function. To create a memoized instance of the function, I simply call the `memoize()` method.

Example 6-12 shows a unit test comparing the invocation of the two approaches.

Example 6-12. Comparing approaches

```
@Test
public void flyweight_computers() {
  def bob = new AssignedComputer(
    ComputerFactory.instance.ofType("MacBookPro6_2"), "Bob")
  def steve = new AssignedComputer(
    ComputerFactory.instance.ofType("MacBookPro6_2"), "Steve")
  assertTrue(bob.computerType == steve.computerType)

  def sally = new AssignedComputer(
    computerOfType("MacBookPro6_2"), "Sally")
  def betty = new AssignedComputer(
    computerOfType("MacBookPro6_2"), "Betty")
  assertTrue sally.computerType == betty.computerType
  }
```

The result is the same, but notice the huge difference in implementation details. For the "traditional" design pattern, I created a new class to act as a factory, implementing two methods. For the functional version, I implemented a single method, then returned a memoized version. Offloading details such as caching to the runtime means fewer opportunities for handwritten implementations to fail. In this case, I preserved the semantics of the Flyweight pattern but with a very simple implementation.

Factory and Currying

In the context of design patterns, currying acts as a factory for functions. A common feature in functional programming languages is first-class (or higher-order) functions, which allow functions to act as any other data structure. Thanks to this feature, I can easily create functions that return other functions based on some criterion, which is the essence of a factory. For example, if you have a general function that adds two numbers, you can use currying as a factory to create a function that always adds one to its parameter—an incrementer, as shown in Example 6-13, implemented in Groovy.

Example 6-13. Currying as a function factory

```
def adder = { x, y -> x + y}
def incrementer = adder.curry(1)

println "increment 7: ${incrementer(7)}"
```

In Example 6-13, I curry the first parameter as 1, returning a function that accepts a single parameter. In essence, I have created a function factory.

I would like to return to an example from an earlier chapter on recursive filtering in Scala, shown in Example 6-14.

Example 6-14. Recursive filtering in Scala

```
object CurryTest extends App {

  def filter(xs: List[Int], p: Int => Boolean): List[Int] =
    if (xs.isEmpty) xs
    else if (p(xs.head)) xs.head :: filter(xs.tail, p)
    else filter(xs.tail, p)

  def dividesBy(n: Int)(x: Int) = ((x % n) == 0) // ❶

  val nums = List(1, 2, 3, 4, 5, 6, 7, 8)
  println(filter(nums, dividesBy(2)))  // ❷
  println(filter(nums, dividesBy(3)))
}
```

❶ A function is defined to be curried.

❷ filter expects as parameters a collection (nums) and a function that accepts a single parameter (the curried dividesBy() function).

What's interesting in Example 6-14 from a patterns standpoint is the "casual" use of currying in the dividesBy() method. Notice that dividesBy() accepts two parameters and returns true or false based on whether the second parameter divides evenly into the first. However, when this method is called as part of the invocation of the fil ter() method, it is called with only one parameter—the result of which is a curried function that is then used as the predicate within the filter() method.

This example illustrates the first two of the ways that patterns manifest in functional programming, as I listed them at the start of this section. First, currying is built into the language or runtime, so the concept of a function factory is ingrained and doesn't require extra structure. Second, it illustrates my point about different implementations. Using currying as in Example 6-14 would likely never occur to typical Java programmers, who have never really had portable code and certainly never thought about constructing specific functions from more general ones. In fact, chances are that most imperative developers wouldn't think of using a design pattern here, because creating a specific dividesBy() method from a general one seems like a small problem, whereas design patterns—relying mostly on structure to solve problems and therefore requiring a lot of overhead to implement—seem like solutions to large problems. Using currying as it was intended doesn't justify the formality of a special name other than the one it already has.

 Use currying to construct *specific* functions from *general* ones.

Structural Versus Functional Reuse

Recall the quote from Chapter 1:

> OO makes code understandable by *encapsulating* moving parts. FP makes code understandable by *minimizing* moving parts.
>
> — Michael Feathers

Working in a particular abstraction every day causes it to seep gradually into your brain, influencing the way you solve problems. In this section, I tackle code reuse via refactoring and the attendant abstraction impact.

One of the goals of object orientation is to make encapsulating and working with state easier. Thus, its abstractions tend toward using state to solve common problems, implying the use of multiple classes and interactions—what Michael Feathers calls "moving parts."

Functional programming tries to minimize moving parts by composing parts together rather than coupling structures together. This is a subtle concept that's hard to see for developers whose primary experience is with object-oriented languages.

Code Reuse Via Structure

The imperative (and especially) object-oriented programming style uses structure and messaging as building blocks. To reuse object-oriented code, you extract the target code into another class, then use inheritance to access it.

To illustrate code reuse and its implications, I return to a version of the now-familiar number classifier to illustrate code structure and style.

You could also write code that uses a positive integer's factors to determine if it is a prime number (defined as an integer greater than 1 whose only factors are 1 and the number itself). Because both of these problems rely on a number's factors, they are good candidates for refactoring (no pun intended) and thus for illustrating styles of code reuse.

Example 6-15 shows the number classifier written in an imperative style.

Example 6-15. Imperative number classifier

```java
public class ClassifierAlpha {
    private int number;

    public ClassifierAlpha(int number) {
        this.number = number;
    }

    public boolean isFactor(int potential_factor) {
        return number % potential_factor == 0;
    }

    public Set<Integer> factors() {
        HashSet<Integer> factors = new HashSet<>();
        for (int i = 1; i <= sqrt(number); i++)
            if (isFactor(i)) {
                factors.add(i);
                factors.add(number / i);
            }
        return factors;
    }

    static public int sum(Set<Integer> factors) {
        Iterator it = factors.iterator();
        int sum = 0;
        while (it.hasNext())
            sum += (Integer) it.next();
        return sum;
    }

    public boolean isPerfect() {
        return sum(factors()) - number == number;
    }

    public boolean isAbundant() {
        return sum(factors()) - number > number;
    }

    public boolean isDeficient() {
        return sum(factors()) - number < number;
    }
}
```

I discuss the derivation of this code in Chapter 2, so I won't repeat it now. Its purpose here is to illustrate code reuse. That leads me to the similar code in Example 6-16, which determines prime numbers.

Example 6-16. Imperative prime number finder

```java
public class PrimeAlpha {
    private int number;

    public PrimeAlpha(int number) {
        this.number = number;
    }

    public boolean isPrime() {
        Set<Integer> primeSet = new HashSet<Integer>() {{
            add(1); add(number);}};
        return number > 1 &&
                factors().equals(primeSet);
    }

    public boolean isFactor(int potential_factor) {
        return number % potential_factor == 0;
    }

    public Set<Integer> factors() {
        HashSet<Integer> factors = new HashSet<>();
        for (int i = 1; i <= sqrt(number); i++)
            if (isFactor(i)) {
                factors.add(i);
                factors.add(number / i);
            }
        return factors;
    }

}
```

A few items of note appear in Example 6-16. The first is the slightly odd initialization code in the `isPrime()` method. This is an example of an instance initializer, a construction quirk in Java that allows me to create instances outside the constructor by placing code blocks within the class but outside any method declarations.

The other items of interest in Example 6-16 are the `isFactor()` and `factors()` methods. Notice that they are identical to their counterparts in the `ClassifierAlpha` class (in Example 6-15). This is the natural outcome of implementing two solutions independently and realizing that you have virtually the same functionality.

Refactoring to eliminate duplication

The solution to this type of duplication is to refactor the code into a single `Factors` class, which appears in Example 6-17.

Example 6-17. Refactored common code

```java
public class FactorsBeta {
    protected int number;
```

```
    public FactorsBeta(int number) {
        this.number = number;
    }

    public boolean isFactor(int potential_factor) {
        return number % potential_factor == 0;
    }

    public Set<Integer> getFactors() {
        HashSet<Integer> factors = new HashSet<>();
        for (int i = 1; i <= sqrt(number); i++)
            if (isFactor(i)) {
                factors.add(i);
                factors.add(number / i);
            }
        return factors;
    }
}
```

The code in Example 6-17 is the result of using *Extract Superclass* refactoring in your IDE of choice. Notice that because both of the extracted methods use the number member variable, it is dragged into the superclass. While performing this refactoring, the IDE asked me how I would like to handle access (accessor pair, protected scope, etc.). I chose *protected scope*, which adds number to the class and creates a constructor to set its value.

Once I've isolated and removed the duplicated code, both the number classifier and the prime number tester are much simpler. Example 6-18 shows the refactored number classifier.

Example 6-18. Refactored, simplified classifier

```
public class ClassifierBeta extends FactorsBeta {

    public ClassifierBeta(int number) {
        super(number);
    }

    public int sum() {
        Iterator it = getFactors().iterator();
        int sum = 0;
        while (it.hasNext())
            sum += (Integer) it.next();
        return sum;
    }

    public boolean isPerfect() {
        return sum() - number == number;
    }

    public boolean isAbundant() {
```

```
        return sum() - number > number;
    }

    public boolean isDeficient() {
        return sum() - number < number;
    }

}
```

Example 6-19 shows the refactored prime number tester.

Example 6-19. Refactored, simplified prime number tester

```
public class PrimeBeta extends FactorsBeta {
    public PrimeBeta(int number) {
        super(number);
    }

    public boolean isPrime() {
        Set<Integer> primeSet = new HashSet<Integer>() {{
            add(1); add(number);}};
        return getFactors().equals(primeSet);
    }

}
```

Regardless of which access option you choose for the number member when refactoring, you must deal with a network of classes when you think about this problem. Often this is a good thing, because it allows you to isolate parts of the problem, but it also has downstream consequences when you make changes to the parent class.

This is an example of code reuse via *coupling*: tying together two elements (in this case, classes) via the shared state of the number field and the getFactors() method from the superclass. In other words, this works by using the built-in coupling rules in the language. Object orientation defines coupled interaction styles (how you access member variables via inheritance, for example), so you have predefined rules about how things are coupled—which is good, because you can reason about behavior in a consistent way. Don't misunderstand me: I'm not suggesting that using inheritance is a bad idea. Rather, I'm suggesting that it is overused in object-oriented languages in lieu of alternative abstractions that have better characteristics.

Code reuse via composition

In Chapter 2, I presented a functional version of the number classifier in Java, shown in Example 6-20.

Example 6-20. More functional version of number classifier

```
import java.util.Collection;
import java.util.Collections;
```

```java
import java.util.HashSet;
import java.util.Set;

public class NumberClassifier {

    public static boolean isFactor(final int candidate, final int number) {    ❶
        return number % candidate == 0;
    }

    public static Set<Integer> factors(final int number) {                      ❷
        Set<Integer> factors = new HashSet<>();
        factors.add(1);
        factors.add(number);
        for (int i = 2; i < number; i++)
            if (isFactor(i, number))
                factors.add(i);
        return factors;
    }

    public static int aliquotSum(final Collection<Integer> factors) {
        int sum = 0;
        int targetNumber = Collections.max(factors);
        for (int n : factors) {                                                 ❸
            sum += n;
        }
        return sum - targetNumber;
    }

    public static boolean isPerfect(final int number) {
        return aliquotSum(factors(number)) == number;
    }
                                                                                ❹
    public static boolean isAbundant(final int number) {
        return aliquotSum(factors(number)) > number;
    }

    public static boolean isDeficient(final int number) {
        return aliquotSum(factors(number)) < number;
    }
}
```

❶ All methods must accept number as a parameter—no internal state exists to hold it.

❷ All methods are public static because they are *pure functions*, thus generically useful outside the number classification realm.

❸ Note the use of the most general reasonable parameter, aiding reuse at the function level.

❹ No caching is present, making this version inefficient for repeating classifications.

I also have a functional version (using pure functions and no shared state) of the Example 6-16, whose isPrime() method appears in Example 6-21. The rest of its code is identical to the same-named methods in Example 6-20.

Example 6-21. Functional version of prime number tester

```
public class FPrime {

    public static boolean isPrime(int number) {
        Set<Integer> factors = Factors.of(number);
        return number > 1 &&
                factors.size() == 2 &&
                factors.contains(1) &&
                factors.contains(number);
    }
}
```

Just as I did with the imperative versions, I extract the duplicated code into its own Factors class, changing the name of the factors() method to of() for readability, as shown in Example 6-22.

Example 6-22. The functional refactored Factors class

```
public class Factors {
    static public boolean isFactor(int number, int potential_factor) {
        return number % potential_factor == 0;
    }

    static public Set<Integer> of(int number) {
        HashSet<Integer> factors = new HashSet<>();
        for (int i = 1; i <= sqrt(number); i++)
            if (isFactor(number, i)) {
                factors.add(i);
                factors.add(number / i);
            }
        return factors;
    }

}
```

Because all the state in the functional version is passed as parameters, no shared state comes along with the extraction. Once I have extracted this class, I can refactor both the functional classifier and prime number tester to use it. Example 6-23 shows the refactored number classifier.

Example 6-23. Refactored number classifier

```
public class FClassifier {

    public static int sumOfFactors(int number) {
        Iterator<Integer> it = Factors.of(number).iterator();
        int sum = 0;
```

```
        while (it.hasNext())
            sum += it.next();
        return sum;
    }

    public static boolean isPerfect(int number) {
        return sumOfFactors(number) - number == number;
    }

    public static boolean isAbundant(int number) {
        return sumOfFactors(number) - number > number;
    }

    public static boolean isDeficient(int number) {
        return sumOfFactors(number) - number < number;
    }
}
```

Note that I didn't use any special libraries or languages to make the second version more functional. Rather, I did it by using *composition* rather than *coupling* for code reuse. Both Examples 6-22 and 6-23 use the Factors class, but its use is entirely contained within individual methods.

The distinction between coupling and composition is subtle but important. In a simple example such as this, you can see the skeleton of the code structure showing through. However, when you end up refactoring a large code base, coupling pops up everywhere because that's one of the reuse mechanisms in object-oriented languages. The difficulty of understanding exuberantly coupled structures has harmed reuse in object-oriented languages, limiting effective reuse to well-defined technical domains such as object-relational mapping and widget libraries. The same level of reuse has eluded us when we write less obviously structured object-oriented code (such as the code you write in business applications).

I could have improved the imperative version by noticing that the IDE is offering to create coupling between the parent and child via a protected member. Rather than introduce coupling, I should use composition instead. Thinking as a more functional programmer means thinking differently about all aspects of coding. Code reuse is an obvious development goal, and imperative abstractions tend to solve that problem differently from the way that functional programmers solve it.

At the beginning of this section, I delineated the ways that design patterns intersect with function programming. First, they can be absorbed by the language or runtime. I showed examples of this using the Factory, Strategy, Singleton, and Template Method patterns. Second, patterns can preserve their semantics but have completely different implementations; I showed an example of the Flyweight pattern using classes versus using memoization. Third, functional languages and runtimes can have wholly different features, allowing them to solve problems in completely different ways.

CHAPTER 7

Practical Thinking

Many of the examples I've featured thus far are abstract, because I'm illustrating the different thinking mode required for functional programming. But at some point you have to take these lessons back to the real world.

In this chapter, I cover some real-world occurrences of functional thinking, starting with Java 8 and moving to functional architectures and web frameworks.

Java 8

I've shown the lambda syntax for Java 8 in numerous examples throughout the book. Rather than merely bolt higher-order functions onto the language, the Java 8 engineers made clever choices to enable older interfaces to take advantage of functional features.

In Chapter 2, I showed an example of the "company process," along with the Java 8 solution, repeated here in Example 7-1.

Example 7-1. Company process in Java 8

```java
public String cleanNames(List<String> names) {
    if (names == null) return "";
    return names
            .stream()
            .filter(name -> name.length() > 1)
            .map(name -> capitalize(name))
            .collect(Collectors.joining(","));
}

private String capitalize(String e) {
    return e.substring(0, 1).toUpperCase() + e.substring(1, e.length());
}
```

With streams in Java 8, you can chain and compose functions together until you call a function that generates output (called a *terminal operation*), such as collect() or forEach(). The `filter()` method in Example 7-1 is the same filter method I've shown throughout the book. The `filter()` method accepts a higher-order function that returns a Boolean value, which is used as the filtering criterion: `true` indicates inclusion in the filtered collection, and `false` indicates absence from the collection.

However, Java has added some syntactic sugar to the language in addition to the functional features. For example, I simplify the lambda block in Example 7-1 from `filter((name) → name.length() > 1)` to the shorter `filter(name → name.length() > 1)`. For single parameters, the superfluous set of parentheses is optional. The return types also sometimes "hide" with the stream.

The `filter()` method accepts a type of `Predicate<T>`, which is a method that returns a Boolean value. You can explicitly create predicate instances if you like, as shown in Example 7-2.

Example 7-2. Creating a predicate manually

```
Predicate<String> p = (name) -> name.startsWith("Mr");
List<String> l = List.of("Mr Rogers", "Ms Robinson", "Mr Ed");
l.stream().filter(p).forEach(i -> System.out.println(i));
```

In Example 7-2, I create a predicate by assigning the filtering lambda block to it. When I call the `filter()` method on the third line, I pass the predicate as the expected parameter.

In Example 7-1, the `map()` method works as expected, applying the `capitalize()` method to each element in the collection. Finally, I call the `collect()` method, which is a terminal operation—a method that generates values from the stream. `collect()` performs the familiar reduce operation: combining elements to produce a (typically) smaller result, sometimes a single value (for example, a sum operation). Java 8 has a `reduce()` method, but `collect()` is preferred in this case because it works efficiently with mutable containers such as a `StringBuilder`.

By adding awareness of functional constructs such as *map* and *reduce* to existing classes and collections, Java faces the issue of efficient collection updates. For example, a *reduce* operation is much less useful if you can't use it on typical Java collections such as `ArrayList`. Many of the collection libraries in Scala and Clojure are immutable by default, which enables the runtime to generate efficient operations. Java 8 cannot force developers to change collections, and many of the existing collection classes in Java are mutable. Therefore, Java 8 includes methods that perform mutable reduction for collections such as `ArrayList` and `StringBuilder` that update existing elements rather than replace the result each time. Although `reduce()` will work in Example 7-1, `collect()` works more efficiently for the collection returned in this instance. Understanding the difference between the two is the overhead with adding sophisticated capabilities to existing languages.

Functional Interfaces

A common Java idiom is an interface with a single method—called a *SAM* (single abstract method) interface—such as `Runnable` or `Callable`. In many cases, SAMs are used primarily as a transport mechanism for portable code. Now, portable code is best implemented in Java 8 with a lambda block. A clever mechanism called *functional interfaces* enables lambdas and SAMs to interact in useful ways. A functional interface is one that includes a single abstract method (and can include several default methods). Functional interfaces augment existing SAM interfaces to allow substitution of traditional anonymous class instances with a lambda block. For example, the `Runnable` interface can now be flagged with the `@FunctionalInterface` annotation. This optional annotation tells the compiler to verify that `Runnable` is an interface (and not a `class` or `enum`) and that the annotated type meets the requirements of a functional interface.

As an example of the substitutability of lambda blocks, I can create a new thread in Java 8 by passing a lambda block in lieu of a `Runnable` anonymous inner class:

```
new Thread(() -> System.out.println("Inside thread")).start();
```

Functional interfaces can seamlessly integrate with lambda blocks in myriad useful places. Functional interfaces are a notable innovation because they work well with established Java idioms.

With Java 8, you can also declare *default methods* on interfaces. A default method is a public nonabstract, nonstatic method (with a body), declared in an interface type and marked with the `default` keyword. Each default method is automatically added to classes that implement the interface—a convenient way to decorate classes with default functionality. For example, the `Comparator` interface now includes more than a dozen default methods. If I create a comparator by using a lambda block, I can trivially create the reverse comparator, as shown in Example 7-3.

Example 7-3. The `Comparator` class's default methods

```
List<Integer> n = List.of(1, 4, 45, 12, 5, 6, 9, 101);
Comparator<Integer> c1 = (x, y) -> x - y;
Comparator<Integer> c2 = c1.reversed();
System.out.println("Smallest = " + n.stream().min(c1).get());
System.out.println("Largest = " + n.stream().min(c2).get());
```

In Example 7-3, I create a `Comparator` instance wrapped around a lambda block. Then, I can create a reverse comparator by calling the `reversed()` default method. The ability to attach default methods to interfaces mimics a common use of *mixins* and is a nice addition to the Java language.

The *mixin* concept is common across several languages. It originated with the Flavors language (*http://bit.ly/wiki-flavors-lang*). The concept was inspired by an ice cream shop near the office where language development occurred. The ice cream parlor offered plain flavors of ice cream with any additional "mixins" (crumbled candy bars, sprinkles, nuts, etc.) that customers wanted.

Some early object-oriented languages defined attributes and methods of class together in a single block of code, whereupon the class definition was complete. In other languages, developers can define the attributes in one place but defer the method definitions until later and "mix" them into the class at the appropriate time. As object-oriented languages evolved, so did the details of how mixins work with modern languages.

In Ruby, Groovy, and similar languages, mixins augment existing class hierarchies as a cross between an interface and parent class. Like interfaces, mixins both act as types for instanceof checks and follow the same extension rule. You can apply an unlimited number of mixins to a class. Unlike interfaces, mixins not only specify the method signatures but also can implement the signatures' behavior. Default methods in Java 8 provide mixins for Java, which allows the JDK to dispense with hacks such as the Arrays and Collections classes, which were nothing but static methods with no homes.

Optional

Notice the trailing call to get() in the terminal calls in Example 7-3. Calls to built-in methods such as min() return an Optional rather than a value in Java 8. This behavior mimics the behavior I discussed in Chapter 5. Optional prevents method returns from conflating null as an error with null as a legitimate value. Terminal operations in Java 8 can use the ifPresent() method to execute a code block only if a legitimate result exists. For example, this code prints the result only if a value is present:

```
n.stream()
    .min((x, y) -> x - y)
    .ifPresent(z -> System.out.println("smallest is " + z));
```

An orElse() method also exists that I can use if I want to take additional action. Browsing the Comparator interface in Java 8 is an illuminating look at how much power default methods add.

Java 8 Streams

Many functional languages and frameworks (such as Functional Java (*http://functional java.org*)) contain a *stream* abstraction, each with subtle differences. Java 8 added streams and supports a nice representative subset of features.

The stream abstraction in Java 8 makes many advanced functional features possible. Streams act in many ways like collections, but with key differences:

- Streams do not store values, but rather act as a pipeline from an input source to a destination through a terminal operation.

- Streams are designed to be functional rather than stateful. For example, the `fil ter()` operation returns a stream of filtered values without modifying the underlying collection.

- Stream operations try to be as lazy as possible (see Chapter 4).

- Streams can be unbounded (or infinite). For example, you can construct a stream that returns all numbers and use methods such as `limit()` and `findFirst()` to gather subsets.

- Like `Iterator` instances, streams are consumed upon use and must be regenerated before subsequent reuse.

Stream operations are either *intermediate* or *terminal* operations. Intermediate operations return a new stream and are always lazy. For example, using a `filter()` operation on a stream doesn't actually filter the stream but rather creates a stream that will only return the filtered values when traversed by a terminal operation. Terminal operations traverse the stream, producing values or side effects (if you write functions that produce side effects, which is discouraged).

Functional Infrastructure

Most of the examples in this book feature advantages of functional programming on a small scale: replacing the Command design pattern with closures, using memoization, and so on. But what about the big pieces that developers must deal with every day, such as databases and software architecture?

Changing from anonymous inner classes to lambda blocks is easy because Java engineers built good solution mechanisms, and they made it easy to change your application piecemeal to use functional constructs. Unfortunately, it's much harder to incrementally change your software architecture or the fundamental way you deal with data. In the next few sections, I explore how functional programming impacts the practical world.

Architecture

Functional architectures embrace immutability at the core level, leveraging it as much as possible. Embracing immutability is high on the list of ways to think like a functional programmer. Although building immutable objects in Java requires a bit more up-front complexity, the downstream simplification forced by this abstraction easily offsets the effort.

Immutable classes make a host of typically worrisome things in Java go away. One of the benefits of switching to a functional mindset is the realization that tests exist to check that changes occur successfully in code. In other words, testing's real purpose is to validate mutation—and the more mutation you have, the more testing is required to make sure you get it right.

There is a direct correlation between mutable state and tests: more of the first requires more of the latter.

If you isolate the places where changes occur by severely restricting mutation, you create a much smaller space for errors to occur and have fewer places to test. Because changes only occur upon construction, immutable classes make it trivial to write unit tests. You do not need a copy constructor, and you need never sweat the gory details of implementing a `clone()` method. Immutable objects make good candidates for use as keys in either maps or sets; keys in dictionary collections in Java cannot change value while being used as a key, so immutable objects make great keys.

Immutable objects are also automatically thread-safe and have no synchronization issues. They can also never exist in unknown or undesirable state because of an exception. Because all initialization occurs at construction time, which is atomic in Java, any exception occurs before you have an object instance. Joshua Bloch calls this *failure atomicity*: success or failure based on mutability is forever resolved once the object is constructed.

To make a Java class immutable, you must:

Make all fields `final`.
> When you define fields as `final` in Java, you must either initialize them at declaration time or in the constructor. Don't panic if your IDE complains that you don't initialize them at the declaration site. It'll realize that you've come back to your senses when you write the appropriate code in the constructor.

Make the class `final` *so that it cannot be overridden.*
> If the class can be overridden, its methods' behaviors can be overridden as well, so your safest bet is to disallow subclassing. Notice that this is the strategy used by Java's `String` class.

Do not provide a no-argument constructor.
> If you have an immutable object, you must set whatever state it will contain in the constructor. If you have no state to set, why do you have an object? Static methods on a stateless class would work just as well. Thus, you should never have a no-argument constructor for an immutable class. If you're using a framework that requires this for some reason, see if you can satisfy it by providing a private no-argument constructor (which is visible via reflection).

> Notice that the lack of a no-argument constructor violates the JavaBeans standard, which insists on a default constructor. But JavaBeans cannot be immutable anyway, because of the way their `setXXX` methods work.

Provide at least one constructor.

If you haven't provided a no-argument one, this is your last chance to add some state to the object!

Do not provide any mutating methods other than the constructor.

Not only must you avoid typical JavaBeans-inspired setXXX methods, but you must also be careful not to return mutable object references. The fact that the object reference is final doesn't mean that you can't change what it points to. Thus, you need to make sure that you defensively copy any object references that you return from getXXX methods.

Groovy has syntactic sugar to handle the gory details of immutablility for you, as shown in Example 7-4.

Example 7-4. An immutable Client class

```
@Immutable
class Client {
    String name, city, state, zip
    String[] streets
}
```

By virtue of using the @Immutable annotation, this class has the following characteristics:

- It is final.
- Properties automatically have private backing fields with get methods synthesized.
- Any attempts to update properties result in a ReadOnlyPropertyException.
- Groovy creates both ordinal and map-based constructors.
- Collection classes are wrapped in appropriate wrappers, and arrays (and other cloneable objects) are cloned.
- Default equals(), hashcode(), and toString() methods are automatically generated.

The @Immutable annotation nicely illustrates my recurring theme: ceding implementation details to the runtime.

Tools such as object-relational mappers unfortunately assume mutable objects in many cases, and either work inefficiently or not at all with immutable objects. Thus, to see pervasive changes toward the functional paradigm will take major changes in many parts of existing systems.

Using a functional language such as Scala or Clojure and their frameworks makes it easier to build systems that embrace functional concepts at a deep level.

Some architectures exist that embrace functional ideals using existing infrastructure, such as *Command-Query Responsibility Segregation* (CQRS).

CQRS

Greg Young (*http://codebetter.com/gregyoung*) introduced the concept of CQRS and Martin Fowler wrote an influential description (*http://bit.ly/fowler-cqrs*) of the concept, which embodies many function aspects.

Traditional application architecture *complects* reading and writing data, typically to a relational database. Developers have expended vast amounts of time and effort to solve the object-relational mapping, with moderate success. Traditional application architecture resembles Figure 7-1.

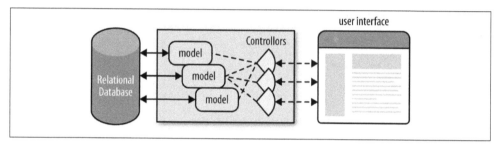

Figure 7-1. Traditional application architecture

The *model* part of the application handles work such as business rules and validations. Typically, model objects also coordinate persistence, either internally or via another logical tier. Developers must consider mixed read and write implications throughout the model, adding complexity.

CQRS simplifies parts of your architecture by separating the *read* and *command* parts of the architecture. In the CQRS world illustrated in Figure 7-2, one part of the model (and perhaps specialized controllers as well) deal with database updates, while other parts of the model handle presentation and reporting.

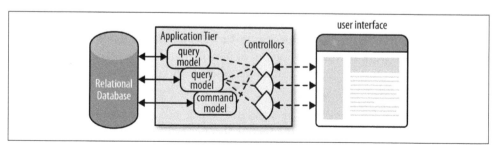

Figure 7-2. CQRS architecture

The logic on the *query* side is typically much simpler because developers can assume immutability; *updates* go through another mechanism. Separate models can imply separate logical processes, perhaps even running on different machines. For example, one set of servers is responsible for display, and the user is routed to another subnet to make changes or additions.

Architecture is always about trade-offs. While making some things easier, CQRS complicates others. For example, if you have a monolithic database, transactions are easy. In CQRS, you will likely need to move to an *eventual consistency* model rather than transactional.

Eventual Consistency

The *eventual consistency* model of distributed computing doesn't require hard time limits on changes to a model but guarantees that, if no new updates occur, the model will eventually be consistent.

Transactions rely on *ACID* (*A*tomic, *C*onsistent, *I*solated, *D*urable), whereas eventual consistency uses *BASE* (*B*asically *A*vailable, *S*oft state, *E*ventual consistency).

Moving away from transactions is often forced as applications must scale. CQRS is a natural fit for architectural patterns such as *event sourcing*, in which you capture all the application state changes as a stream of events. Separating *read* from *mutate* allows for simpler logic; for example, everything on the *read* side can be immutable.

Web Frameworks

No discussion of new languages or paradigms is complete until the subject of web frameworks is addressed. Web programming is a terrific fit for functional programming: one can view the entire Web as a series of transformations from request to response.

Every functional language has a variety of web frameworks, with varying degrees of popularity. They all have most of these characteristics in common:

Routing frameworks
   Most modern web application frameworks, including functional web frameworks, utilize routing libraries to decouple routing details from application functionality. Often, routing information is kept in a standard data structure (e.g., a Vector inside another Vector) that libraries know how to traverse.

Functions as targets
   Many functional web applications use functions as the target for routing destinations. It's easy to think about a web request as a function that accepts a Request and

returns a `Response`; some portion of functional web frameworks represents syntactic sugar around this plumbing.

DSLs

Martin Fowler defines DSLs as computer programming languages of limited expressiveness, focused on a narrow problem domain. A popular type of DSL is an *internal* DSL, a new pseudolanguage written atop another language, using stylized syntactic sugar of the host language. The Ruby on Rails (*http://rubyonrails.org*) web framework and C#'s LINQ (*http://bit.ly/ms-linq*) are good examples of this approach.

Most modern web frameworks use DSLs in several locations, including routing, embedded elements in HTML, database interaction, and so on. Use of DSLs is a common approach across a wide variety of languages, but functional languages in particlar favor declarative code, often the goal of DSLs.

Tight integration with build tools

Rather than being tethered to an IDE, most functional web frameworks have tight integration with command-line build tools, using them for everything from generating new project structure to running tests. IDEs and editors alike can automate around the existing tool chains, but the coupling between build tools and artifact production is tight, making it hard to rebuild.

As with all general-purpose languages, some parts of web development with functional languages will be easier and some will be harder. In general, coding with more immutable values cuts down on your testing burden: less state transition to verify via tests. Once you can establish conventions (such as immutability) throughout your architecture, it becomes easier for each piece to cooperate.

Databases

What is the motivation for relational databases doing destructive updates? In other words, every time you do a database update, you destroy the old value when you replace it with the new. Why are databases designed this way? To maximize storage space, so that your data won't continue to grow. This architectural decision was embedded into database design decades ago, yet the landscape has changed. Resources (particularly virtual ones) are cheap now—Amazon will rent them to you for pennies! Yet developers still endure the pains imposed by the architectural constraints of yesteryear.

The Clojure community (*http://clojure.org*) has been slowly building tools to support functional architectures from the browser down to the persistence tier. Datomic (*http://www.datomic.com*), the Clojure community's entry into the commercial NoSQL database world, is particularly interesting because it is an example of how far designers can push functional concepts when they suffuse the entire architecture.

Datomic is an immutable database that timestamps each fact as it is entered. As the Datomic documentation observes, when President Obama took office, it didn't mean that President Bush had never been president. By storing *values* rather than *data*, Datomic uses space quite efficiently. Once a value has been entered, all other instances of that value can point to the original (which can never change because it is immutable), making space usage efficient. If you need to update what your application sees at some point in the future, you can point to another value. Datomic has added the concept of time to information, allowing facts to always remain in their proper context.

Several interesting implications fall out of this design:

Permanent recording of all schema and data changes
Everything (including schema manipulation) is retained, making it trivial to migrate to an earlier version of your database. An entire category of tools (database migration tools) exists to solve this problem for relational databases.

Separation of reads and writes
Datomic's architecture naturally separates *read* and *write* operations, meaning that updates are never delayed by queries. Thus, Datomic is architecturally a CQRS system internally.

Immutability and timestamps for event-driven architectures
Event-driven architectures rely on a stream of events to capture application state change. A database that captures and timestamps each piece of information is ideally suited, allowing rewind and playback as a feature of the database.

Datomic is just one example of the kinds of tools that developers will be able to create once they can cast off previous constraints and start building tools and frameworks with a deep paradigm change toward functional programming.

CHAPTER 8

Polyglot and Polyparadigm

Functional programming is a programming paradigm, a framework for thinking a certain way about problems and the attendant tools to implement that vision. Many modern languages are *polyparadigm* (or *multiparadigm*): they support a number of different programming paradigms, such as object orientation, metaprogramming, functional, procedural, and many more.

Groovy is a multiparadigm language: it supports object orientation, metaprogramming, and functional programming styles, which are mostly orthogonal to one another. Metaprogramming allows you to add features to a language and its core libraries. By combining metaprogramming with functional programming, you can make your own code more functional or augment third-party functional libraries to make them work better in Groovy. In the next section, I show how to use metaprogramming via the `Expando MetaClass` to weave a third-party functional library (Functional Java) seemingly into the core of Groovy.

Orthogonality

The definition of *orthogonal* spans several disciplines, including mathematics and computer science. In math, two vectors that are at right angles to each other are orthogonal, meaning that they never intersect. In computer science, orthogonal components don't have any effects (or side effects) on one another. For example, functional programming and metaprogramming are orthogonal in Groovy because they don't interfere with each other: using metaprogramming doesn't restrict you from using functional constructs, and vice versa. The fact that they are orthogonal doesn't mean that they can't work together, merely that they don't interfere with each other.

Combining Functional with Metaprogramming

By now, you're quite familiar with my number classification example. While useful, it still exists as a separate function. Perhaps number classification is key to my business, and I would like it woven into the programming language itself, for convenience. In Groovy, the `ExpandoMetaClass` allows me to add methods to existing classes, including existing language classes. To make `Integer` classifier aware, I add the methods to `Integer`, as shown in Example 8-1, assuming the functional version of my number classifier from Chapter 2.

Example 8-1. Using metaprogramming to make `Integer` *classifier aware*

```
Integer.metaClass.isPerfect = {->
  Classifier.isPerfect(delegate)
}

Integer.metaClass.isAbundant = {->
  Classifier.isAbundant(delegate)
}

Integer.metaClass.isDeficient = {->
  Classifier.isDeficient(delegate)
}
```

In Example 8-1, I add the three `Classifier` methods to `Integer`. Now, all integers in Groovy have these methods. Groovy has no notion of primitive data types; even constants in Groovy use `Integer` as the underlying data type. Within the code block defining each method, I have access to the predefined `delegate` parameter, which represents the value of the object that is invoking the method on the class.

> ## Initializing Metaprogramming Methods
>
> You must add metaprogramming methods before the first attempt to invoke them. The safest place to initialize them is in the static initializer for the class that uses them (because it's guaranteed to run before other initializers for the class), but this adds complexity when multiple classes need augmented methods. Generally, applications that use a lot of metaprogramming end up with a bootstrap class to ensure that initialization occurs at the appropriate time.

Once I've initialized my metaprogramming methods, I can "ask" numbers about categories:

```
assertTrue num.isDeficient()
assertTrue 6.isPerfect()
```

The newly added methods work on both variables and constants. It would now be trivial to add a method to `Integer` that returns the classification of a particular number, perhaps as an enumeration.

Adding new methods to existing classes isn't in itself particularly "functional," even if the code they call is strongly functional. However, the ability to add methods seamlessly makes it easy to incorporate third-party libraries—such as the Functional Java library (*http://functionaljava.org*)—that add significant functional features.

Mapping Data Types with Metaprogramming

Groovy is essentially a dialect of Java, so pulling in third-party libraries such as Functional Java is trivial. However, I can further weave those libraries into Groovy by performing some metaprogramming mapping between data types to make the seams less visible. Groovy has a native closure type (using the `Closure` class). Functional Java doesn't have the luxury of closures yet (it relies on Java 5 syntax), forcing the authors to use generics and a general `F` class that contains an `f()` method. Using the Groovy `ExpandoMetaClass`, I can resolve the method/closure type differences by creating mapping methods between the two.

I augment the `Stream` class from Functional Java (*http://functionaljava.org*), which provides an abstraction for infinite lists, to enable passing Groovy closures in place of Functional Java `F` instances. To implement this weaving, I add overloaded methods to the `Stream` class to map closures into F's `f()` method, as shown in Example 8-2.

Example 8-2. Mapping Functional Java classes into collections via metaprogramming

```
  static {
    Stream.metaClass.filter = { c -> delegate.filter(c as fj.F) }
//    Stream.metaClass.filter = { Closure c -> delegate.filter(c as fj.F) }
    Stream.metaClass.getAt = { n -> delegate.index(n) }
    Stream.metaClass.getAt = { Range r -> r.collect { delegate.index(it) } }
  }

  @Test
  void adding_methods_to_fj_classes() {
    def evens = Stream.range(0).filter { it % 2 == 0 }
    assertTrue(evens.take(5).asList() == [0, 2, 4, 6, 8])
    assertTrue((8..12).collect { evens[it] } == [16, 18, 20, 22, 24])
    assertTrue(evens[3..6] == [6, 8, 10, 12])
  }
```

The first line in Example 8-2 creates a `filter()` method on `Stream` that accepts a closure (the c parameter of the code block). The second (commented) line is the same as the first, but with the added type declaration for the `Closure`; it doesn't affect how Groovy executes the code but might be preferable as documentation. The body of the code block calls `Stream`'s preexisting `filter()` method, mapping the Groovy closure to the Functional Java `fj.F` class. I use Groovy's semimagical `as` operator to perform the mapping.

Groovy's `as` operator coerces closures into interface definitions, allowing the closure methods to map to methods required by the interface. Consider the code in Example 8-3.

Example 8-3. Groovy's as operator coerces maps into interface implementations

```
h = [hasNext: { h.i > 0 }, next: {h.i--}]
h.i = 10    // ❶
def pseudoIterator = h as Iterator    // ❷

while (pseudoIterator.hasNext())
  print pseudoIterator.next() + (pseudoIterator.hasNext() ? ", " : "\n")
// 10, 9, 8, 7, 6, 5, 4, 3, 2, 1,
```

❶   A map's closures can refer to other members of the map.

❷   as generates an implementation.

In Example 8-3, I create a hash with two name-value pairs. Each of the names is a string (Groovy doesn't require hash keys to be delimited with double quotes, because they are strings by default), and the values are code blocks. The `as` operator maps this hash to the `Iterator` interface, which requires both `hasNext()` and `next()` methods. Once I've performed the mapping, I can treat the hash as an iterator; the last line of the listing prints true. In cases in which I have a single-method interface or when I want all the methods in the interface to map to a single closure, I can dispense with the hash and use `as` directly to map a closure onto a function. Referring back to the first line of Example 8-2, I map the passed closure to the single-method F class. In Example 8-2, I must map both `getAt()` methods (one that accepts a number and another that accepts a `Range`) because filter needs those methods to operate.

Using this newly augmented `Stream`, I can play around with an infinite sequence, as shown in the tests at the bottom of Example 8-2. I create an infinite list of even integers, starting with 0, by filtering them with a closure block. You can't get all of an infinite sequence at once, so you must `take()` as many elements as you want. The remainder of Example 8-2 shows testing assertions that demonstrate how the stream works.

Infinite Streams with Functional Java and Groovy

In Chapter 4, I showed how to implement a lazy infinite list in Groovy. Rather than create it by hand, why not rely on an infinite sequence from Functional Java?

To create an infinite `Stream` of perfect numbers, I need two additional `Stream` method mappings to understand Groovy closures, as shown in Example 8-4.

Example 8-4. Two additional method mappings for perfect-number stream

```
static {
  Stream.metaClass.asList = { delegate.toCollection().asList() }
//   Stream.metaClass.static.cons =
//     { head, Closure c -> delegate.cons(head, ['_1':c] as fj.P1)}
  Stream.metaClass.static.cons =
    { head, closure -> delegate.cons(head, closure as fj.P1) }
}
```

In Example 8-4, I create an `asList()` conversion method to make it easy to convert a Functional Java `Stream` to a list. The other method that I implement is an overloaded `cons()`, which is the method on `Stream` that constructs a new list. When an infinite list is created, the data structure typically contains a first element and a closure block as the tail of the list, which generates the next element when invoked. For my Groovy stream of perfect numbers, I need Functional Java to understand that `cons()` can accept a Groovy closure.

If I use `as` to map a single closure onto an interface that has multiple methods, that closure is executed for any method I call on the interface. That style of simple mapping works in most cases for Functional Java classes. However, a few methods require a `fj.P1()` method rather than a `fj.F` method. In some of those cases, I can still get away with a simple mapping because the downstream methods don't rely on any of the other methods of `P1`. In cases in which more precision is required, I may have to use the more complex mapping shown in the commented line in Example 8-4, which must create a hash with the `_1()` method mapped to the closure. Although that method looks odd, it's a standard method on the `fj.P1` class that returns the first element.

Once I have my metaprogrammatically mapped methods on `Stream`, I add to the Groovy implementation of `Classifier` to create an infinite stream of perfect numbers, as shown in Example 8-5.

Example 8-5. Infinite stream of perfect numbers using Functional Java and Groovy

```
def perfectNumbers(num) {
  cons(nextPerfectNumberFrom(num), { perfectNumbers(nextPerfectNumberFrom(num))})
}

@Test
void infinite_stream_of_perfect_nums_using_funtional_java() {
  assertEquals([6, 28, 496], perfectNumbers(1).take(3).asList())
}
```

I use static imports both for Functional Java's `cons()` and for my own `nextPerfectNum berFrom()` method from `Classifier` to make the code less verbose. The `perfectNum bers()` method returns an infinite sequence of perfect numbers by `cons`ing (yes, `cons` is a verb) the first perfect number after the seed number as the first element and adding a closure block as the second element. The closure block returns the infinite sequence with the next number as the head and the closure to calculate yet another one as the tail. In the test, I generate a stream of perfect numbers starting from 1, taking the next three perfect numbers and asserting that they match the list.

When developers think of metaprogramming, they usually think only of their own code, not of augmenting someone else's. Groovy allows me to add new methods not only to built-in classes such as `Integer`, but also to third-party libraries such as Functional Java. Combining metaprogramming and functional programming leads to great power with very little code, creating a seamless link.

Although I can call Functional Java classes directly from Groovy, many of the library's building blocks are clumsy when compared to real closures. By using metaprogramming, I can map the Functional Java methods to allow them to understand convenient Groovy data structures, achieving the best of both worlds. As projects become more polyglot, developers frequently need to perform similar mappings between language types: a Groovy closure and a Scala closure aren't the same thing at the bytecode level. Having a standard in Java 8 will push these conversations down to the runtime and eliminate the need for mappings like the ones I've shown here. Until that time, though, this facility makes for clean yet powerful code.

Consequences of Multiparadigm Languages

Multiparadigm languages offer immense power, allowing developers to mix and match suitable paradigms. Many developers chafe at the limitations in Java prior to version 8, and a language such as Groovy provides many more facilities, including metaprogramming and functional constructs.

While powerful, multiparadigm languages require more developer discipline on large projects. Because the language supports many different abstractions and philosophies, isolated groups of developers can create starkly different variants in libraries. As I illustrated in Chapter 6, fundamental considerations differ across paradigms. For example, code reuse tends toward *structure* in the object-oriented world, whereas it tends toward *composition* and *higher-order functions* in the functional world. When designing your company's `Customer` API, which style will you use? Many developers who moved from Java to Ruby encountered this problem, because Ruby is a forgiving multiparadigm language.

One solution relies on engineering discipline to ensure that all developers are working toward the same goal. Unit testing enables pinpoint understanding of complex extensions via metaprogramming. Techniques such as consumer-driven contracts allow developers to create contracts (in the form of tests) that act as executable contracts between teams.

Consumer-Driven Contracts

A consumer-driven contract (*http://bit.ly/fowler-consumer-driven-contract*) is a set of tests agreed upon by both an integration provider and supplier(s). The provider "agrees" that it will run the tests as part of its regular build and ensure that all the tests remain *green*. The tests ensure the assumptions between the various interested parties. If either party needs to make a breaking change, all the affected parties get together and agree on an upgraded set of tests. Thus, consumer-driven contracts provide an executable integration safety net that requires coordination only when things must evolve.

Many C++ projects suffered from awkwardly spanning procedural and object-orientation programming styles Fortunately, modern engineering practices and exposure to the dangers in multiparadigm languages can help.

Some languages solve this problem by primarily embracing one paradigm while pragmatically supporting others. For example, Clojure is firmly a functional Lisp for the JVM. It allows you to interact with classes and methods from the underlying platform (and create your own if you like), but its primary support is for strongly functional paradigms such as immutability and laziness. Clojure doesn't obviate the need for engineering disciplines like testing, but its idiomatic use doesn't stray far from Clojure's specific design goals.

Context Versus Composition

Functional thinking pervades more than just the languages you use on projects. It affects the design of tools as well. In Chapter 6, I defined *composition* as a design ethos in the functional programming world. Here I want to apply that same idea to tools and contrast two abstractions prevalent in the development world: *composable* and *contextual*. Plug-in-based architectures are excellent examples of the *contextual* abstraction. The plug-in API provides a plethora of data structures and other useful context that developers inherit from or summon via already existing methods. But to use the API, a developer must *understand* what that context provides, and that understanding is sometimes expensive. I ask developers how often they make nontrivial changes to the way their editor/IDE behaves beyond the preferences dialog. Heavy IDE users do this much less frequently, because extending a tool like Eclipse takes an immense amount of knowledge. The knowledge and effort required for a seemingly trivial change prevents the change from occurring, leaving the developer with a perpetually dull tool. Contextual tools aren't bad things at all—Eclipse and IntelliJ wouldn't exist without that approach. Contextual tools provide a huge amount of infrastructure that developers don't have to build. Once mastered, the intricacies of Eclipse's API provide access to enormous encapsulated power. And there's the rub: how encapsulated?

In the late 1990s, 4GLs (*http://bit.ly/wiki-4gl*) were all the rage, and they exemplified the contextual approach. They built the context into the language itself: dBASE, FoxPro, Clipper, Paradox, PowerBuilder, Microsoft Access, and their ilk all had database-inspired facilities directly in the language and tooling. Ultimately, 4GLs fell from grace because of *Dietzler's Law*, which I define in my book *The Productive Programmer* (O'Reilly), based on experiences of my colleague Terry Dietzler, who ran the Access projects for my employer at the time.

Dietzler's Law for Access

Every Access project will eventually fail because, while 80% of what the user wants is fast and easy to create, and the next 10% is possible with difficulty, ultimately the last 10% is impossible because you can't get far enough underneath the built-in abstractions, and *users always want 100% of what they want.*

Ultimately, Dietzler's Law killed the market for 4GLs. Although they made it easy to build simple things fast, they didn't scale to meet the demands of the real world. We all returned to general-purpose languages.

Composable systems tend to consist of fine-grained parts that are expected to be wired together in specific ways. Powerful exemplars of this abstraction show up in Unix shells with the ability to chain disparate behaviors together to create new things. In Chapter 1, I alluded to a famous story from 1992 (*http://bit.ly/more-shell-less-egg*) that illustrates how powerful these abstractions are. Donald Knuth was asked to write a program to solve this text-handling problem: *read a file of text, determine the n most frequently used words, and print out a sorted list of those words along with their frequencies.* He wrote a program consisting of more than 10 pages of Pascal, designing (and documenting) a new algorithm along the way. Then, Doug McIlroy demonstrated a shell script that would easily fit within a Twitter post that solved the problem more simply, elegantly, and understandably (if you understand shell commands):

```
tr -cs A-Za-z '\n' |
tr A-Z a-z |
sort |
uniq -c |
sort -rn |
sed ${1}q
```

I suspect that even the designers of Unix shells are often surprised at the inventive uses developers have wrought with their simple but powerfully composable abstractions.

Contextual systems provide more scaffolding, better out-of-the-box behavior, and contextual intelligence via that scaffolding. Thus, contextual systems tend to ease the friction of initial use by doing more for you. Huge global data structures sometimes hide behind inheritance in these systems, creating a huge footprint that shows up in derived extensions via their parents. Composable systems have less implicit behavior and initial ease of use but tend to provide more granular building blocks that lead to more eventual power. Well-designed composable systems provide narrow local context within encapsulated modules.

These abstractions apply to tools and frameworks as well—particularly tools that must scale in their power and sophistication along with projects, such as build tools. By hard-won lessons, *composable build tools scale (in time, complexity, and usefulness) better than contextual ones.* Contextual tools such as Ant and Maven allow extension via a plug-in API, making extensions that the original authors envisioned easy. However, trying to extend it in ways not designed into the API range in difficulty from hard to impossible: Dietzler's Law redux. This is especially true with tools in which critical parts of how they function, such as the ordering of tasks, are inaccessible without hacking.

This is why every project eventually hates Maven. Maven is a classic contextual tool: it is opinionated, rigid, generic, and dogmatic, *which is exactly what is needed at the beginning of a project.* Before anything exists, it's nice for something to impose a structure and to make it trivial to add behavior via plug-ins and other prebuilt niceties. But over time, the project becomes less generic and more like a real, messy project. Early on, when no one knows enough to have opinions about things such as life cycle, a rigid system is good. Over time, though, project complexity requires developers to spawn opinions, and tools like Maven don't care.

Tools built atop languages tend to be more composable. My all-time favorite build language for personal and project work (almost without regard to the project technology stack) is Rake (*http://rake.rubyforge.org*), the build tool in the Ruby world. It is a fantastic combination of simplicity and power. When I first migrated from Ant to Rake, I started poking around the Rake documentation to find out which tasks are available in Rake, hoping to find something simliar to the giant list of tasks (and extensions) familiar in the Ant world. I was disgusted by the lack of documentation until I realized that there wasn't any for a reason: you can do anything you need within Rake tasks, because it's just Ruby code. Rake has added some nice helpers for file list manipulation, but Rake mostly just handles tasks dependencies and housekeeping, getting out of the way of developers.

People will accuse me of bashing Maven, but I'm actually not—I'm trying to foster understanding for when it's useful. No tool works perfectly in every context, and much grief visits projects that try to use tools outside their expiration date. Maven is perfect for starting new projects: it ensures consistency and provides a huge bang for the buck in terms of existing functionality. But the fact that something starts strong doesn't mean that it scales well. (In fact, almost always the opposite is true.) The real trick is to use Maven until the day it starts fighting you, then find an alternative. Once you start fighting with Maven, it'll never return to the rosy days when your relationship was young.

Fortunately, at least one Maven get-out-of-jail-free card exists in Gradle (*http:// www.gradle.org*), which still understands the Maven stuff you already have, but is language-based rather than plug-in–based—implemented as a Groovy domain-specific language—making it more composable than Maven.

Many contextualized systems eventually become more composable by being redesigned as DSLs. Consider the 4GLs from the 1990s. Ruby on Rails and similar frameworks are just like those 4GLs, with a critical distinction: they are implemented as internal DSLs *atop* a general-purpose language. When developers in those environments hit the upper percentages of Dietzler's Law, they can drop below the framework back to the underlying general-purpose language. Rake and Gradle are both DSLs, and I've come to believe that scripting builds is far too specific and unique to each project to use contextualized tools.

Functional Pyramid

Computer language types generally exist along two axes, pitting strong versus weak and dynamic versus static, as shown in Figure 8-1.

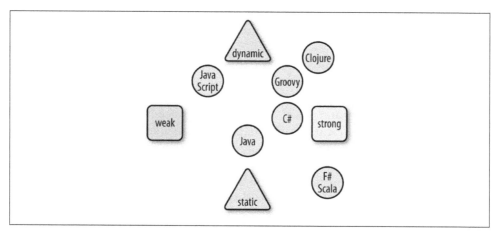

Figure 8-1. Language categories

Static typing indicates that you must specify types for variables and functions beforehand, whereas dynamic typing allows you to defer it. Strongly typed variables "know" their type, allowing reflection and instance checks, and they retain that knowledge. Weakly typed languages have less sense of what they point to. For example, C is a statically, weakly typed language: variables in C are really just a collection of bits that can be interpreted in a variety of ways, to the joy and horror (sometimes simultaneously) of C developers everywhere.

Java is strongly, statically typed: you must specify variable types, sometimes several times over, when declaring variables. Scala, C#, and F# are also strongly, statically typed but manage with much less verbosity by using type inference. Many times, the language can discern the appropriate type, allowing for less redundancy.

The diagram in Figure 8-1 is not new; this distinction has existed as long as languages have been studied. However, a new aspect has entered into the equation: *functional programming*.

As I've shown throughout this book, functional programming languages have a different design philosophy than imperative ones. Imperative languages try to make mutating state easier and have lots of features for that purpose. Functional languages try to minimize mutable state and build more general-purpose machinery.

But functional doesn't dictate a typing system, as you can see in Figure 8-2.

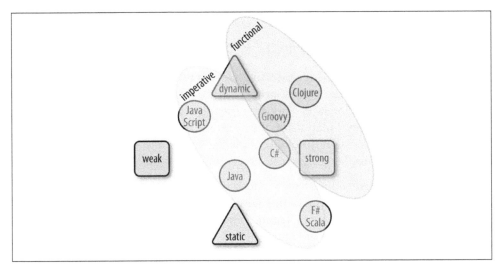

Figure 8-2. Languages with paradigm overlay

With the added reliance—even insistence—on immutability, the key differentiator among languages now isn't dynamic versus static, but imperative versus functional, with interesting implications for the way we build software.

On my blog back in 2006, I accidentally repopularized the term polyglot programming (*http://bit.ly/ford-polyglot-programming*) and gave it a new meaning: taking advantage of modern runtimes to create applications that mix and match languages but not platforms. This was based on the realization that the Java and .NET platforms support more than 200 languages between them, with the added suspicion that there is no One True Language that can solve every problem. With modern managed runtimes, you can freely mix and match languages at the byte code level, utilizing the best one for a particular job.

After I published my article, my colleague Ola Bini published a follow-up paper discussing his Polyglot Pyramid, which suggests the way people might architect applications in the polyglot world, as shown in Figure 8-3.

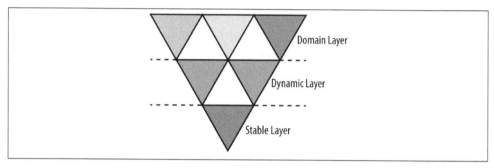

Figure 8-3. Ola Bini's polyglot language pyramid

In Bini's original pyramid, he suggests using more static languages at the bottommost layers, where reliability is the highest priority. Next, he suggests using more dynamic languages for the application layers, utilizing friendlier and simpler syntax for building things like user interfaces. Finally, atop the heap, are DSLs, built by developers to succinctly encapsulate important domain knowledge and workflow. Typically, DSLs are implemented in dynamic languages to leverage some of their capabilities in this regard.

This pyramid was a tremendous insight added to my original post, but upon reflection about current events, I've modified it. I now believe that typing is a red herring that distracts from the important characteristic, which is functional versus imperative. My new Polyglot Pyramid appears in Figure 8-4.

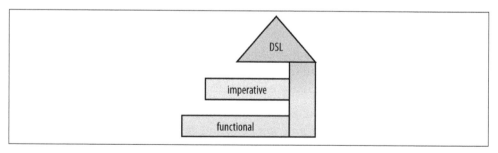

Figure 8-4. My functional pyramid

I believe that the resiliency we crave comes not from static typing but from embracing functional concepts at the bottom. If all of your core APIs for heavy lifting—data access,

---

integration—could assume immutability, all that code would be much simpler. Of course, it would change the way we build databases and other infrastructure, but the end result will be guaranteed stability at the core.

Atop the functional core, use imperative languages to handle workflow, business rules, user interfaces, and other parts of the system for which developer productivity is a priority. As in the original pyramid, DSLs sit on top, serving the same purpose. However, I also believe that DSLs will penetrate through all the layers of our systems, all the way to the bottom. This is exemplified by the ease with which you can write DSLs in languages like Scala (functional, statically strongly types) and Clojure (functional, dynamically strongly typed) to capture important concepts in concise ways.

This is a huge change, but it has fascinating implications. Rather than stress about dynamic versus static, the much more interesting discussion now is functional versus imperative, and the implications of this change go deeper than the arguments about *static* versus *dynamic*. In the past, we designed imperatively using a variety of languages. Switching to the functional style is a bigger shift than just learning a new syntax, but the beneficial effects can be profound.

Index

Symbols

4GLs (fourth-generation programming languages), 152

A

Abstract Factory design pattern, 86, 89
Abstract Syntax Tree (AST), 82
abstractions
    benefits of higher-level, 16
    benefits of layers, 40
    composable vs. contextual, 151
Access projects, 152
accumulators, 29
ACID (Atomic, Consistent, Isolated, Durable), 141
aliquot sum, 17
anonymous inner classes, 41

B

BASE (Basically Available, Soft state, Eventual), 141
Bini, Ola, 156
Bloch, Joshua, 138
bytecode, 5

C

caching
    caching everything, 62
    caching sum, 60
    function-level, 59
    intraclass, 60
    method-level, 60
case classes, 108
catamorphism, 29
Clojure
    built-in list-comprehension, 84
    currying/partial application in, 47
    filter variants in, 34
    fold/reduce variants in, 38
    functional programming example in, 14
    laziness in, 80
    map operation in, 28
    map variants in, 36
    memoization in, 68
    multimethods/polymorphism in, 89
    optimization for maps, 85
    parallel processing in, 16
    readable code in, 88
    traversing tree-shaped structures in, 85
closures, 40–44
code reuse
    refactoring, 126
    structure vs. composition, 150
    via composition, 128

We'd like to hear your suggestions for improving our indexes. Send email to index@oreilly.com.

J

Java
error handling in, 96
inflexibility of, 85
keywords in, 88
lazy iterator in, 70
making classes immutable, 138
number classifier in, 17
switch statement in, 86
Java 8
default methods, 135
filtering in, 25
functional features for older interfaces, 133
functional interfaces, 135
functional programming example in, 13
mixins in, 136
number classifier in, 21
Optional, 136
parallel processing, 16
streams, 136
streams/work reordering in, 56
JUnit testing framework, 73

K

keywords, 88

L

lambda blocks, 21
language trends
composable vs. contextual abstractions, 151
dispatch options
Clojure's Lisp code, 88
Clojure's multimethods/polymorphism,
89
improving with Groovy, 86
dynamic vs. static typing, 154, 157
few data structures/many operations, 83
focus on solutions, 85
functional data structures
Either class, 97
Either trees, 108
error handling, 96
Option class, 105
overview of, 95
imperative vs. functional, 155, 157
operator overloading
in Groovy, 91

in Scala, 93
orthogonality, 145
poly- and multiparadigm, 145, 150
laziness
benefits of, 70, 80
definition of, 70
lazy field initialization, 82
lazy iterator in Java, 70
lazy lists in Groovy, 74–79
Totally Lazy framework, 72
lazy parsing, 102
Lisp code, 88

M

map operation
illustration of, 25
in Clojure, 28
in Groovy, 27
synonyms for in Clojure, 36
synonyms for in Groovy, 35
synonyms for in Scala, 34
Maven, 153
Memento Pattern, 115
memoization
adding, 63–69
caching
caching everything, 62
caching sum, 60
method-level, 60
Flyweight design pattern, 119
usefulness of, 59
metafunctions, 63
metaprogramming
benefits of, 145
combining with functional, 146, 150
infinite streams, 148
initializing, 146
mapping data types with, 147
method-level caching, 60
Michie, Donald, 59
mixin concept, 136
multimethods, 89
multiparadigm languages, 145, 150
multithreaded code, 40

N

nonstrict evaluation, 70
null errors, 136

number classification
    categories of, 17
    functional, 19
    imperative, 17
    in Functional Java, 22
    in Java 8, 21
    optimized Clojure version, 28
    optimized Groovy version, 27
    optimized imperative version, 26

O

object-oriented programming (OOP)
    code reuse in, 6, 83, 114
    common constructs in, 5
    implementing factory functions in, 51
Option class, 105
orthogonality, 145

P

parallel processing
    in Clojure, 16
    in Java 8, 16
    in Scala, 16
partial (constrained) functions, 48
partial application (see currying/partial application)
partial functions, 49
pattern matching, 48, 86, 106
perfect numbers problem, 17
performance optimization
    adding memoization, 63–69
    caching, 60–63
    lazy evaluation, 70–82
Polyglot Pyramid, 156
polymorphism, 89
polyparadigm languages, 145
The Productive Programmer (Ford), 152
pure functions, 59, 95

R

recursion, 52–56
reduce/fold operations
    in Functional Java, 29
    in Groovy, 30
    left/right folds, 30
    similarities and differences in, 29
refactoring, 126

referential transparency, 96
resiliency, 157

S

SAM (single abstract method) interface, 135
Scala
    case classes in, 108
    currying/partial application in, 45, 47
    Either class in, 97
    filter variants in, 32
    flexibility of, 85
    fold/reduce variants in, 36
    functional programming example in, 13
    laziness in, 81
    map variants in, 34
    memoization in, 69
    operator overloading in, 93
    parallel processing in, 16
    partial (constrained) functions in, 48
    partially applied functions in, 48
    pattern matching in, 106
    recursive filtering in, 55
stack growth, 56
static typing, 154, 157
Strategy design pattern, 118
streams, 136, 148
streams/work reordering, 56
strict evaluation, 70
switch statement, 86

T

tail-call optimization, 56
Template Method design pattern, 51, 116
terminal operations, 134, 137
thread-last macro, 15, 28
Totally Lazy framework, 72

U

union data type, 97

V

values, 95
virtual machines, 5

W

web frameworks
    domain-specific languages (DSLs), 142
    functions as targets, 142
    routing frameworks, 141
    tight integration with build tools, 142
work reordering/streams, 56
Working with Legacy Code (Feathers), 5
wrapping exceptions, 104

X

XML, parsing in Clojure, 84

Y

Young, Greg, 140

Z

zipper data structure, 85

About the Author

Neal Ford is Director, Software Architect, and Meme Wrangler at ThoughtWorks, a global IT consultancy with an exclusive focus on end-to-end software development and delivery. Before joining ThoughtWorks, Neal was the Chief Technology Officer at The DSW Group, Ltd., a nationally recognized training and development firm. Neal has a degree in computer science from Georgia State University specializing in languages and compilers and a minor in mathematics specializing in statistical analysis. He is also the designer and developer of applications, instructional materials, magazine articles, video presentations, and author of *Developing with Delphi: Object-Oriented Techniques* (Prentice-Hall, 1996), *JBuilder 3 Unleashed* (Sams, 1999; as the lead author), *Art of Java Web Development* (Manning, 2003), *The Productive Programmer* (O'Reilly, 2008), *Presentation Patterns* (Pearson, 2012), and numerous anthologies. Neal's primary consulting focus is the design and construction of large-scale enterprise applications. He is also an internationally acclaimed speaker, having spoken at numerous developer conferences worldwide. If you have an insatiable curiosity about Neal, visit his website (*http://www.nealford.com*). He welcomes feedback and can be reached at *nford@thoughtworks.com*.

Colophon

The animal on the cover of *Functional Thinking* is a thick-tailed greater galago (of the *Otolemur* genus), also known as a thick-tailed bushbaby. These primates are native to southern and eastern Africa. Galagos are mostly arboreal, and prefer tropical and subtropical forest habitat, though they can occasionally be found in woodland savannah.

These animals have thick brown or gray fur, large ears and eyes, and long tails to help with balance as they travel through the trees. They are also equipped with long fingers and toes tipped with thickened skin pads to grasp limbs. On average, they are a foot long (not including the tail) and weigh 2–3 pounds.

The thick-tailed greater galago is nocturnal; during the day, it rests 5–12 meters above the ground, concealed within a dense nest of vines in a tree hollow. They are generally solitary, and mark their territories with a scent gland in their chest as well as urine (though male territories often overlap with those of females).

At night, galagos come out to forage for food. They are agile and able to make short jumps from tree to tree, though they usually just walk unless alarmed. They eat fruit, seeds, acacia gum, flowers, and insects. Biologists have observed that each individual animal spends nearly half of each evening traveling and only 20% foraging, and often patrols the same route each night.

The cover image is from Cassell's *Natural History*. The cover fonts are URW Typewriter and Guardian Sans. The text font is Adobe Minion Pro; the heading font is Adobe Myriad Condensed; and the code font is Dalton Maag's Ubuntu Mono.

Have it your way.

Get even more for your money.

Join the O'Reilly Community, and register the O'Reilly books you own. It's free, and you'll get:

- $4.99 ebook upgrade offer
- 40% upgrade offer on O'Reilly print books
- Membership discounts on books and events
- Free lifetime updates to ebooks and videos
- Multiple ebook formats, DRM FREE
- Participation in the O'Reilly community
- Newsletters
- Account management
- 100% Satisfaction Guarantee

Signing up is easy:

1. Go to: oreilly.com/go/register
2. Create an O'Reilly login.
3. Provide your address.
4. Register your books.

Note: English-language books only

To order books online:
oreilly.com/store

For questions about products or an order:
orders@oreilly.com

To sign up to get topic-specific email announcements and/or news about upcoming books, conferences, special offers, and new technologies:
elists@oreilly.com

For technical questions about book content:
booktech@oreilly.com

To submit new book proposals to our editors:
proposals@oreilly.com

O'Reilly books are available in multiple DRM-free ebook formats. For more information:
oreilly.com/ebooks

O'REILLY®